JOHN CALVIN

Father of Reformed Theology

Sam Wellman

BARBOUR BOOKS

An Imprint of Barbour Publishing, Inc.

Other books in the "Heroes of the Faith" series:

Brother Andrew
Saint Augustine
Gladys Aylward
Dietrich Bonhoeffer
William and Catherine Booth
John Bunyan
John Calvin
William Carey
Amy Carmichael
George Washington Carver
Fanny Crosby
Frederick Douglass
Jonathan Edwards
Jim Elliot
Charles Finney
Billy Graham
C. S. Lewis
Eric Liddell
David Livingstone
Martin Luther
D. L. Moody
Samuel Morris

George Müller
Watchman Nee
John Newton
Florence Nightingale
Luis Palau
Francis and Edith Schaeffer
Charles Sheldon
Mary Slessor
Charles Spurgeon
John and Betty Stam
Billy Sunday
Hudson Taylor
William Tyndale
Corrie ten Boom
Mother Teresa
Sojourner Truth
John Wesley
George Whitefield
William Wilberforce
John Wycliffe
Some Gave All

© 2001 by Sam Wellman.

ISBN 1-58660-298-5

Published by Barbour Books, an imprint of Barbour Publishing, Inc., P.O. Box 719, Uhrichsville, OH 44683, www.barbourbooks.com

Cover illustration © Dick Bobnick.

ecpa Member of the
Evangelical Christian
Publishers Association

Printed in the United States of America.
5 4 3

JOHN CALVIN

one

John Calvin was six years old in 1515. He lived in the small French town of Noyon, about one hundred miles north of Paris. A town as small and remote as Noyon should have been as peaceful and uneventful as its mild climate. But it was not. It had a great cathedral and a palace for its bishop because the bishop of Noyon was a powerful man. In fact, the bishop was one of just twelve peers under the king who ruled all of France. For hundreds of years, Noyon had drawn great makers of history. The king who became the greatest king in all the history of France—Charlemagne—had been crowned king of Nuestra there in A.D. 768. The king who founded the long-running Capetian dynasty—Hugh Capet—had been crowned there in A.D. 987.

"Noyon is no insignificant place," said John Calvin's father, who was secretary to the powerful bishop of Noyon.

John's father, Gerard—who was about fifty years old—was astute and energetic. Gerard had risen far above his own father's station. Grandfather Calvin was a maker of barrels for wine. He lived just two miles away in Pont l'Évêque, which in French meant "bridge of the bishop" because a bridge spanned the Oise River there. Despite fringing willow trees draping wispy branches down on the river, the Oise was not a welcoming river. The Oise was deeply incised in clay banks, so it could sweep a wader into nightmarish, deadly places with no hope of climbing out. At one time Grandfather Calvin had been a boatman on the river. Produce from the fertile area around Noyon could be taken all the way to Paris on boats. So Grandfather Calvin had seen a thing or two. And although he remained in Pont l'Évêque, all his sons—perhaps spurred by his tales of other places—had moved elsewhere. Gerard's brother—John's uncle Richard—had even taken his iron-working skills from Pont l'Évêque to Paris, where he had become a locksmith.

But in Noyon, John's father was forever trying to arrange future income for his three sons through the church. These arrangements were called *benefices*. Gerard had already arranged a future chaplaincy at the cathedral for John's older brother Charles. The benefice would support him in modest comfort. Gerard was trying hard to get John a partial chaplaincy. Time was crucial; Gerard had heard King Francis I—though he was newly crowned—was as domineering and power hungry as his contemporary, England's Henry VIII. Francis I was trying to get more and more involved in benefices. In the near future, perhaps only friends of the king's friends might receive such monetary blessings.

"Antoine might get nothing," sighed the whispers about John's toddling brother.

John's mother, Joan, was the daughter of the wealthy merchant Le Franc of Cambrai. But Grandfather Le Franc was retired and lived next to the Grain Market in Noyon, just as John and his family did. The Calvins lived in an unpretentious but roomy house between the rue des Porcelets and the rue Fromentiere. To John, his mother was radiant and attentive. She once had a reputation as a beauty. But John heard cynics say that women were goddesses before marriage and servants forever after. Everything he saw confirmed that cynicism. Except for church activities Joan labored constantly. She cleaned, she laundered, she cooked, and she toiled in the garden. Hardworking people of the Calvin class ate vegetables and very little meat. Women served bread and soups stocked with cabbage, carrots, lettuce, lima beans, and potatoes.

"Do you know your Latin for today's lessons, John?" asked his mother.

That question jolted John back into his immediate world. He attended school. In fact, people called it the School of Capettes—not to honor Hugh Capet but to acknowledge the small capes the students wore. Much instruction was in Latin. Latin was the language of the Mass, the Catholic worship service conducted by the priest. Latin was the language of the Holy Bible of John's church, not that he had ever been allowed to read it. Latin was the language of important, educated people all over the world, Gerard told John.

"Non scholae sed vitae discimus," his father emphasized in Latin.

"It is not for school, but for life, that we learn," translated John.

Every morning, except Saturday and Sunday, John and
Charles left their home near the Grain Market to trudge down
the cobbled streets toward the school. It was in the same
direction as Pont l'Évêque where Grandfather Calvin lived
along the Oise River. The streets in Noyon were narrow,
edged by two- and three-story buildings. Above their red-tiled
or gray-slated roofs, John could see steeples and towers, for
Noyon had four parish churches, two monasteries, the
bishop's palace—and most of all, of course, the great twin-
towered, long-backed cathedral of Notre Dame. Like any
town of significance in those days, Noyon had the protection
of outer walls, though its walls were not formidable for 1515.
Within those walls, John's world seemed compact and simple.

"Home, school, and church are my world," he might
have reflected.

Their parish church was Sainte-Godeberte, named after
a seventh-century holy woman of Noyon. A priest had baptized John there—just days after his birth on July 10, 1509—
under the watchful eyes of his godfather, Jean des Vatines,
one of the canons, or elders, of the cathedral. Many memories of this church were vivid for John later in life, although
by then he saw much in them he had missed as a boy. "I
remember seeing as a little boy what happened to the images
in our parish church," he wrote many years later. "On the
feast of Saint Stephen people decorated with chaplets and
ribbons not only the image of the saint himself, but also

those of the tyrants (to give them a common name) who stoned him. When the credulous women saw the tyrants dressed up like this, they took them for companions of the saint and burned a candle for each one. . ."[1]

But at the time John was just as trusting. His mother made church very comfortable and interesting for him. Often they would travel to one of the other churches or monasteries without Gerard for a special occasion. One such occasion was at the Ourscamp Abbey. It was here that the monks claimed to have an unimaginably valuable treasure: a fragment of a bone from the body of Saint Anne, the grandmother of Jesus through Mary. John was allowed to kiss the relic. The thought that the bone might not be authentic never occurred to him at the time.

John learned from his mother that Saint Medard had brought Christianity to Noyon in the sixth century. The son of Roman nobility, Medard first became bishop of Vermand. For greater protection, he moved his bishopric a few miles south to the fortified site of Noyon. He lived to be ninety. The faithful of Noyon revered Medard, but unfortunately for them, Benedictine monks moved the body of Medard to Soissons thirty miles away. There the monks built their monastery over his tomb. Still, Saint Medard was called upon for protection in bad weather and for the relief of toothaches—both no doubt as the result of numerous legends about the saint.

"However, Noyon does have its own buried saint," said John's mother, "Saint Eligius."

Eligius followed Medard by about one century. Eligius was a man of many talents. He became a master goldsmith and designed a jewel-studded throne for King Clotaire II.

He endeared himself to Clotaire II and his son Dagobert. After Dagobert took the throne, Eligius became his chief counselor. He negotiated peace treaties, ransomed prisoners, and started monasteries and churches. It seemed there was nothing he could not accomplish. He began to live as a monk obeying the rules of the Irish saint Columbanus. At forty-nine he became a priest. A year later in A.D. 640 he was bishop of Noyon. He then distinguished himself by converting the Flemings and other barbarian tribes along the sea coast to the north. In Noyon he established a convent for nuns. The bishop died in A.D. 660 at seventy. He became the patron of goldsmiths and all other metalworkers. Not only did some of the writings of Eligius still exist in John's time, but he—not Medard—was the patron saint of Noyon's great cathedral.

Life as a Catholic was so intertwined within the other elements of John Calvin's life that he accepted it as readily as eating or sleeping. He was often active in the church without realizing it. Learning church songs and chants in school seemed a relief from the tyranny of regular lessons. These songs and chants—used during the Mass—were named simply for the first word in their text. He learned in Latin the "Confiteor," the "general confession" chanted at the beginning of Mass. *"Confiteor Deo omnipotenti,"*—I confess to Almighty God—it began. John also memorized the "Sanctus," a short Latin chant from the Book of Isaiah in praise of God. He learned the "Benedictus"—the song of Zechariah in the Book of Luke. Another song John mastered from Luke was the "Magnificat," in praise of Mary, the mother of Jesus. And of course he acquired the "Agnus Dei."

"Agnus Dei, qui tollis peccata mundi, miserere nobis!" chanted the worshippers.

Lamb of God, who takes away the sins of the world, have mercy on us! thought John to himself. At the age of six, John was already beyond the beginners' level in school because of all the rudimentary Latin he had learned. The children had Bible stories in school, too. They not only sang but learned the theory of music. John learned to sing many psalms in Latin. But mastering these songs was not just a school exercise, for when John was older he would become a member of the choir during church rituals. And how frequent they were. The morning Mass was called laud. The evening Mass was vespers. An even later Mass, compline, closed the day.

"Are all these rituals of worship in the sacred Bible?" John asked.

"Well, they must be," replied his mother with surprise.

John was curious, but no one encouraged him to read the Bible. It was the book the priests read. Yet, John and his fellow students had grammar books in Latin. Their text for Latin was one that had been used for hundreds of years. It was called *Donatus.* Actually there were two of them. The "Ars minor"—or "little textbook"—taught basic grammar by means of questions and answers. More advanced students moved on to the "Ars major"—"big textbook"—which taught not only grammar but the subtleties of good writing. The books were printed by a machine. John learned that far to the east in Rhineland, only about fifty years before John was born, a German named Gutenberg had invented a machine that printed books. Men no longer had to laboriously make copies of books by hand. Someone told John that Bibles

11

printed in Latin by machines were now available in great numbers. Perhaps someday he could read one.

But John's world was not only wonder but worry, too. His mother often appeared near collapse. Death was everywhere. Infants suddenly sputtered out like tiny candles. Even thriving, laughing children suddenly fevered and expired. The most terrifying specter was the Black Death, also known as the plague. Black Death was no longer something that happened back in the thirteen hundreds. It had reappeared. It struck somewhere in the France of John's time about every third year. Its occurrence was erratic enough that no year could ever be assumed plague free. No one understood why it appeared or how it spread. Nor could the severity in a particular outbreak be predicted. Perhaps it would take only a few victims. Perhaps it would take tens, hundreds, even thousands.

The heart froze any time someone described a sickness as, "Headache, nausea, vomiting, aching joints. . ."

Those were the early symptoms of the plague!

If the sick person then began to flame with fever, everyone really began to worry. The question of the plague was never in doubt for long. Soon lumps the size of hen eggs swelled and ached in the groin or the armpit or on the neck of the victim. Death was swift. Within four days, terror-stricken workers carted the poor victim away, to be buried in some notorious remote ground for carriers of the pestilence. It was called the Black Death because in the last hours—when the victim wheezed futilely for breath—the skin darkened to a purple hue.

So death worried John in 1515.

Take anyone but Mother, he prayed.

two

B ut death took John's mother. Suddenly she was
gone. Death had taken the dearest life he knew. It
seemed the only way he could accept the fact was
by imagining her in paradise. If he had remained at the
family home near the Grain Market, he might have brooded
along with his father and his brothers. Perhaps his faith
would have crumbled. His brother Charles already whispered his own doubts. But abruptly, John found himself in
the residence of the Montmors, so called because Louis
d'Hangest was the seigneur or count of Montmor.

There were three d'Hangest brothers—Louis, Charles,
and Adrien. Charles was the bishop of Noyon. The brothers
were not only members of the powerful d'Hangest family but
sons of the sister of George de' Amboise. Though Amboise
had died in 1510, he had been an extremely powerful figure

in France. He was the first minister under King Louis XII, predecessor of Francis I. Amboise had been no figurehead either. He had reduced royal spending, and because of that he was able to reduce taxes. He also reformed the judiciary. He helped organize Louis XII's military campaigns. He had become a cardinal and had very nearly become pope.

These revelations of immense power associated with the d'Hangest household nearly overwhelmed John, even though he was a young child, for he was very perceptive. But why was John's brother Charles not there, too?

"You will see older brother Charles at the School of Capettes," explained John's father. "Besides, Charles is nearly ready to assume one of the chaplaincies at the cathedral."

Yet, that did not seem to answer John's question. Why was he the only one of the Calvin brothers at the Montmors'? And there he was tutored right along with all the d'Hangest boys. Of the d'Hangest boys, John was especially close to Claude, one of Adrien's sons.

"Am I here because your family wants to help out my father during this rough time?" John asked Claude.

"Of course not. Do you see Charles or Antoine here?" Claude was brutally frank. "You've been chosen because of your exceptional promise as a student."

The d'Hangest family doted on John. For all their faults, the rich were generous in some ways. If a student showed exceptional promise, they did not squelch his ambitions but tried to advance them. John learned more than Latin there, too. He learned much about the bishop of Noyon. John heard that since the current bishop had assumed his position in

1501, he had feuded with the fifty-seven canons or elders of the church. This group of townsmen was also called the chapter. There were differing opinions within the Catholic Church on the respective roles of the bishop and the cathedral chapter. Some considered the bishop and chapter one body but directed by the bishop. Others considered the chapter as forming a body distinct from the bishop, with its own regulations and interests.

"The bishop of Noyon and his chapter have never resolved this dispute," whispered John's privileged friends.

Because of his presence among wealthy, learned people, John's young ears heard things that boys who lived around the Grain Market did not know at all. How many local citizens knew the beloved Maid of Orléans—Joan of Arc—had been imprisoned in Noyon for a time in 1430? Virtually none. And they would not have believed John if he had told them. For the church at Noyon and its bishop had supported not France in that incident but England! *If only the locals had helped her escape,* thought John. English intruders would have been chased from northern France long before they were finally expelled in 1453. Yet, the rich could wink about such things.

In 1516, when John turned seven, Noyon continued its claim on history. Representatives of Francis I—the king of France—and Charles V—the king of Spain—were negotiating a treaty there. Francis I, just newly crowned in 1515, had personally led a French army across the Alps and defeated the Italians to claim the region of Lombardy. Oddly enough, this territory had been under the rule of Charles V and Spain. Francis I thought France had a claim on the territory of

Naples, too, which Charles V also ruled. To prevent further war, Charles V was going to relinquish Lombardy if Francis was willing to give up any claim on Naples. Even at the age of seven, John Calvin realized these two men were two of the chief rivals for control of Europe.

"And their representatives are right here negotiating," buzzed Noyon in 1516.

Because of his presence among the privileged, John also was well aware that that same year King Francis I had concluded a pact with Pope Leo X. It was just as his father feared. The king gained much control over church appointments in exchange for allowing Rome to take more revenue from France. The church of Rome was always, it seemed, seeking more money for its grandiose plans. Because of Gerard's influence with the bishop, John at least had seemed assured of receiving positions within the church like Charles had received. Now there was some doubt. Just how far would Francis I reach in his control of church appointments?

These events, unknown to the common people, scared John. Sometimes he thought that if Claude had not been such a good friend he might have bolted the confines of the rich d'Hangest household and never returned. He was frightened most of the time anyway because he never knew if his manners were appropriate. All these exalted people were at the very least counts and countesses, presently or in the future.

"Your Grace," John would reply in a thin voice to members of the family or one of their visitors, praying he had used the right form of address.

In the d'Hangest home, John constantly witnessed the

luxuries of the wealthy. They drank the best wines, ate the most expensive cuisine. Vegetables were scorned in favor of beef, venison, poultry, rabbit, pork, cheese, and rich gravies. They dined on gleaming porcelain plates with silver utensils. They had thousands of leather-bound books shelved on gleaming oak and cherry. They had elegant furniture of polished wood and cushioned fabrics. They did not play the ubiquitous stringed lute of the common people, but they mastered the most ingenious new musical instruments. The harpsichord with its stops and couplers to enhance the humming strings was a must for wealthy families who wanted to stay in fashion. Or so John overheard. Claude showed him the latest rage.

"Printed music sheets!" gasped John.

Then in 1517 a curious thing happened.

An entourage from Rome arrived on the outskirts of Noyon with great fanfare. John watched in wonder as priests, magistrates, town officials—and yes, also his father—joined the entourage. Shoulder to shoulder they all marched down the street past the cathedral under banners proclaiming the arrival of these messengers from Rome. Horns tooted and drums thumped. Finally, in the town square, a priest—he appeared to John to be a Franciscan or a Dominican monk—mounted a wooden platform and preached. By that time it seemed everyone in Noyon had gathered in the square. He promised an indulgence—forgiveness of punishment for all sins—for a donation. This forgiveness came directly from Pope Leo X! Donors would not leave empty-handed, either.

"Will my forgiveness be documented in a letter from the Holy Father himself?" cried a man immersed in the crowd of gawking people. John noted that this man was not local, but, in fact, had arrived with the entourage.

The priest solemnly nodded his assent.

"Will it carry the seal of his holiness, Leo X?" another such stranger cried.

Of course, nodded the priest agreeably. He waved gracefully to tables that had been set up away from his platform. John noted with astonishment how these tables, even small tents, had appeared so quickly. His father stood by one of the tables. Nothing scared people in 1517 worse than the thought of eternal damnation in hell. Even the holding tank for all souls, known as purgatory in the Catholic Church, was terrifying. No sin, however revolting—even against the Holy Mother, preached this priest from Rome—would not be forgiven during this special time of indulgences. Eyes blinked in amazement. People surged to the tables with their money. Yet some hesitated.

Then the priest from Rome went into future sins. Money today bought forgiveness tomorrow. Who, if they had the money, could pass that up? More crowded to the tables, trying not to smile too much at the pleasant thought of their future sins. Then the priest began on the past. Yes, perhaps these sinners had purchased their own escape from purgatory but what of their dead parents and grandparents? Had they thought about them in purgatory—that dank world of the dead that sits neither in heaven nor in hell?

"Do you not hear your dead parents crying out, 'Have mercy upon us'?" shouted the priest emotionally. He cupped his hands behind his ears. "Do you not hear, 'We are in sore pain and you can set us free for a mere pittance. We have borne you, we have trained and educated you, we have left you all our property, and you are so hard-hearted and cruel, that you leave us to roast in the flames when you could so easily release us?' "[1]

Surely John's mother wasn't crying out from purgatory, was she? The thought tore at John's heart. If that appeal didn't work nothing would, he thought with his newfound cynicism. There were few indeed who could resist the imagined cries of dead loved ones sitting on the brink of hellfire. Mother. Father. Grandmother. Grandfather. John lingered by the tables. Forgiveness and remission of punishment for sins came at a price, in fact a specific price. This wasn't just some temporary remission. This was a plenary remission from the Pope Leo X himself. Total. Absolute. One could hardly expect such a gift for a few copper coins. A tradesman or craftsman received this boon of a lifetime for gold or much silver. A merchant was expected to pay more. And who could imagine what compensation was expected from nobility like the d'Hangests?

John watched the flurry of activity. Sinners—past, present, and future—now jostled each other in their rush to line up before the clerks' tables. It seemed a challenge for the men at the tables to take in all the money. Several of the entourage—including his father—did nothing but stand and watch the tables with steely eyes. Later that evening—after the entourage from Rome hastily departed—John had the opportunity to ask his father what he had been doing at the tables.

"Representing the interests of the bishop," he said sourly. "Gold and silver coins can so easily be slipped into the sleeve of a tunic, inside a boot. . ."

"But what if a poor peasant had no gold or silver?" blurted John, remembering contrite, trembling peasants in the mob.

His father laughed. "Then the poor soul was hustled inside one of the tents. Our friends from Rome wanted no one with money to see that papal forgiveness could be purchased for a few copper coins."

Later, at the residence of the Montmors, John listened to the d'Hangest boys ask impertinent questions. "But what is the reason for this sudden storm of activity?" one asked.

"We only do the bidding of his holiness Pope Leo X," replied one of the adults angrily. "His holiness has only been pope since 1513. He inherited massive debts from his predecessor Julius II. Julius commissioned a colossal dome—a 'basilica' the arrogant Italians call it—atop St. Peter's Cathedral in Rome. Julius also commissioned the artists Michelangelo and Raphael to paint the walls in his Rome residence, the Vatican. Julius commissioned this, and Julius commissioned that. He even commissioned wars. Then he died. Now good Pope Leo X has to pay for all those commissions." One of the nobles added irrationally, "And how is Leo X to conduct his own war against the Turks without money?"

Later Claude winked at John and whispered, "And my uncle the bishop gets a nice cut for himself."

A few days later in the Montmor household, John heard someone recite a sarcastic ditty: "As soon as the money in the coffer rings, the soul from purgatory's fire springs."[2]

John was sickened. He learned that the tables collecting

20

the money had been manned not only with the religious but with government officials and banking clerks, too. The mounds of money had to be handled properly. Several entities divided the money. The pope's cut was the highest. But King Francis I got a sizeable cut. And, of course, the bishop of Noyon received a portion large enough to "sanction" the selling of indulgences. Think of the poor Germans, the adults laughed in the Montmor household. Even though they were called the Holy Roman Empire and ruled by an emperor, they were not a strong unified nation like England or France or Spain run by kings and queens. The pope must have really been fleecing that patchwork of German-speaking provinces loosely run by an emperor, a bevy of princes, and every other kind of local authority.

But how can this peculiar practice of selling indulgences happen, wondered John to himself, *without someone being very angry about it?*

Nevertheless, John became more and more comfortable with the d'Hangest family and their distinguished friends. He was becoming almost as skilled at the social graces as his friend Claude. These skills were absolutely essential in the France of his time for any opportunity to realize lofty ambitions. Years later he would dedicate a book to Claude saying, "I owe you all that I am. . . As a boy I was brought up in your home and was initiated in my studies with you. Hence, I owe to your noble family my first training in life and letters."[3]

Nor did John disappoint the d'Hangest family. He excelled in his studies. As a scholar, he outperformed Claude and anyone else that he knew. In fact, to his surprise he discovered many called him a genius. By 1521 John, only twelve, received a partial chaplaincy at the cathedral. He was a one-third partner in the altar of La Gesine—that is, "the Nativity"—in Noyon Cathedral. For this, he earned a small stipend for performing minor duties in the cathedral.

The entry in the chapter registers read:

> *19 May, 1521. M. Jaques Regnard, secretary to the Reverend Father in God, Monsignor Charles d'Hangest, Bishop of Noyon, reported to the Chapter that the Vicars General of the said Monsignor had given to John Calvin, son of Gerard, aged twelve years, a portion of the Chapel of La Gesine. . . .[4]*

The reality of a partnership in the cathedral thrilled John. He looked at the great cathedral with new eyes. The church had begun to raise the structure in 1150 and had worked on it ever since. It was over three hundred feet long and about seventy feet wide. The two great square towers fronting the cathedral on the west were not twins as he always assumed. No, they were twins in external form only. The apertures were deliberately different. Whereas one tower had four, the other had three. But ornamentation was subdued. The great size with minimal ornamentation made the cathedral appear particularly massive and marked it as early Gothic in style.

His wealthy friends informed him that cathedrals everywhere ran their main axis, or nave, from west to east. The entrance was on the west end, just as in Noyon. The east end ended in the altar, which tradition said faced the Holy Land. Spoking off the east end were chapels. Siding the nave was the clerestory. This wall stepped down to another wall on the side aisles, then this wall stepped down yet again to the walls of the chapels. So viewing the cathedral from outside the east end, John saw "stair steps." The great nave walls were supported by thick vertical columns, or buttresses. John was told other cathedrals had elegant arched supports called flying buttresses.

On the street, the towers appeared almost short and stumpy next to the long nave. But John discovered this proportionality meant nothing when one climbed up into the bell loft at the top of one of the towers. There the height, to a boy trembling among five bells that could erupt into a soulsearing crescendo, was heavenly. Who would have believed one could see the towers of Châateau Cloucy across the forested plain to the east? Cloucy was a good ten miles away. And the Oise, so hidden within in its deep banks when one was below, could be seen snaking across the green countryside to both horizons. Was this what God's angels saw?

What twelve-year-old would not be enchanted to be linked to one of the chapels of this enormous holy structure? John was marked now as a cleric, too, for he received the tonsure—that shaved crown on top of the head that monks and priests show to God. Now everyone—and most importantly John's father—assumed John was destined to enter study for the priesthood. But where would John go for study and ordination? Would he be allowed somehow to go to Paris? For now, when the Montmors spoke of sending all the d'Hangest boys off to get the best education possible, it was only Paris they spoke of.

"Paris," sighed John. "I've never been anywhere."

John found the world intensely interesting. It promised to be an age of great change. As some had suspected, the selling of indulgences in the German-speaking provinces to the east had run afoul. The indulgence-seller had been a particularly aggressive Dominican friar named Tetzel. It seemed some obscure Augustinian monk in Wittenberg had protested. Tetzel exploded with indignation. He complained to the pope. The pope had sent a representative to chastise the monk. But the representative had run into a firestorm of resentment among a majority of Germans against the practice of indulgences. Then the obscure Augustinian monk was summoned before a cardinal in Augsburg, an important ecclesiastical town near Munich. The cardinal ordered him to recant his protest. The monk defied him. In an earlier time, the monk would have been hastily executed. But Maximilian—the emperor of the Holy Roman Empire, which was roughly all the German-speaking areas—was in very poor health. Because he wanted the support of the German princes to assure that his grandson, Charles V of Spain, would succeed him as emperor of the Holy Roman Empire, he did not want to offend any German prince. And the prince who seemed to be defending this unruly monk was the highly respected Frederick the Wise, also of Wittenberg.

"So the monk was spared," whispered people.

Widely circulating throughout Europe was a compendium of the monk's tracts on the subject of indulgences. He aimed one tract called *Answer to Prieras*—at the pope's hand-picked defender of indulgences. The monk wrote it in 1519 when John was ten:

> *I am sorry now that I despised Tetzel.*
> *Ridiculous as he was, he was more acute than*
> *you. You cite no Scripture. You give no reasons.*
> *Like an insidious devil you pervert the Scriptures.*
> *You say that the Church consists virtually in the*
> *pope. What abominations will you not have to*
> *regard as the deeds of the Church? Look at the*
> *ghastly shedding of blood by Julius II. Look at the*
> *outrageous tyranny of Boniface VIII, who, as the*
> *proverb declares, "came in as a wolf, reigned as a*
> *lion, and died as a dog.". . . You call me a leper*
> *because I mingle truth with error. I am glad you*
> *admit there is some truth. You make the pope into*
> *an emperor in power and violence. The Emperor*
> *Maximilian and the Germans will not tolerate*
> *this. . . .*[5]

When Maximilian died in 1519, Charles V did indeed become the new emperor. But the monk's mission was not finished. In 1520, the fiery monk burned in public a reprimand from the pope. And he didn't stop there. He also burned all the canon law of the church! Early in 1521, the new emperor summoned the monk to their annual meeting of princes called a "diet." It convened in the town of Worms. Again the monk defied authority. No, he would not recant anything he had said or written. Because the emperor did not want to take on Frederick the Wise so publicly, he let the monk go—temporarily, thought the cynics. Then he would be murdered. And indeed the monk disappeared. Had he been murdered? Or was he in hiding somewhere?

His Latin writings were now widely circulated. Their very titles were inflammatory. *The Address to the Christian Nobility of the German Nation on the Improvement of the Christian Estate* seemed to sound the call for a powerful German nation. *On the Babylonian Captivity of the Church* apparently expounded on the abuses of certain powers in the church. And what person fluent in Latin—and that included virtually every educated man and woman in Europe—did not want to at least peek at the tract the monk titled *On the Freedom of a Christian Man*? Catholics—loyalists and rogues alike—felt like the monk's tracts were hot coals threatening to inflame the Catholic world.

Did the young John Calvin hear the writings of the fiery German monk read aloud by titillated members of the d'Hangest family? Perhaps not. But surely he heard many murmurs about this stormy force. No one could recall having ever heard such a strong—and, a few admitted secretly, convincing—voice against the church of Rome. Surely the monk raised intriguing questions. Just what was in the Holy Scriptures? Certainly the church encouraged no one to read them. Many educated Europeans began to wonder what the Scriptures actually said. And the name of the Augustinian monk was on the lips of every educated person in Europe.

"Martin Luther," they murmured.

three

Y ou are going to Paris to study," said Gerard to John
one day.

Gerard had prospered. He was now procurator of
the cathedral chapter, as well as the bishop's secretary.
How he managed to represent both the chapter and the
bishop was puzzling. Because John knew they squabbled.
But Gerard seemed almost a stranger now to John. The
Calvin household was strange, too. Young brother Antoine
gawked at him. John had been out of the household about
half his own life. Most of his memories were in the home
of the d'Hangests. Gerard had remarried. He and his new
wife had two daughters. John watched Gerard's wife—a
virtual stranger—working and primping their modest
dresses. Yes, the Calvin household near the Grain Market
seemed alien to John. But John had no illusions. He knew

that he still answered to Gerard. And apparently Gerard had decided that John was going to Paris.

"You will live with your uncle Richard," Gerard informed him. "He lives near the great church of Saint Germain l'Auxerrois, on the north bank of the Seine River. You will be tutored for preparation for the priesthood."

Paris, with some three hundred thousand inhabitants, was the largest city in Europe in the 1520s. It was said only Constantinople rivaled it in population. Forests of oak and beech rimmed the compact city, which seemed to sit down in a depression. The Seine River entered the city at its southeast corner, flowed northwestward, then arced gradually southwestward and left Paris at its southwest corner. Walls of massive stone blocks contained the river in its course. Great iron rings in the wall were used to moor vessels.

Uncle Richard lived in the heart of the city on the north side of the river. His neighborhood was indeed dominated by the church of Saint Germain l'Auxerrois. The cathedral had only one tower but was far more complex than the cathedral in Noyon. It was also more ornate, that is, more Gothic. Gargoyles leered and scowled down from every vantage point. Royalty attended masses there, so the church was often mentioned as a landmark. If John needed any reminder that this was Paris and not Noyon, the tower erupted with the carol of not five bells but a symphony of thirty-eight!

John could cross the Seine River at the Pont au Change, the "Bridge of Money Changers" that was lined with money changers and goldsmiths and their shops, to set foot on the great island in the Seine called the Île de la Cité. It was the heart of the city, harboring both the royal palace on the west end and the great cathedral of Notre Dame on the east end. However, existing as well on the Île de la Cité in that complex of royalty, nobility, and clergy were the poor unfortunates imprisoned in the dreaded Conciergerie. Parliament met near the royal palace in the Great Hall. Sainte-Chapelle abutted the royal palace like frosting on the cake. King Louis IX built the elegant church in the twelve hundreds to house his treasure of holy relics. At a cost greater than the cost of the construction of the church itself, Louis IX had acquired what were claimed to be Christ's crown of thorns, two pieces of the true cross, a nail from the cross, the Roman soldier's lance that pierced Christ's side, and several drops of Christ's blood. Though King Louis IX later died on one of the crusades, his accomplishments were worthy enough to earn him the title of Saint Louis.

Many among the nobility collected relics very competitively. "It seems every hair on the Holy Mother's head has been saved, every nail in the cross, every bone of every apostle," said John's Paris friends and added with a wink, "Perhaps several times over?"

But whether or not John's circle of privileged friends accepted Louis IX's relics as valid, Sainte-Chapelle was greatly renowned for other reasons. The nave was enormously tall without the aid of flying buttresses. The interior had two tiers. Most of the royal court worshipped on the ground floor, which displayed statues of the twelve disciples. Royalty ascended a spiral staircase to worship high among the relics housed there in gold cases. This upper Chapelle Haute was brightened through a complex of stained glass windows adorning the upper tier. Visitors called it a "jewel box." Only reds and blues were commonly available in the earliest days of stained glass. So the inside from all angles seemed red and blue dyed glass, except the greens and yellows radiating from one great "rose" window above the entrance to the cathedral. The many scenes in the glass were illuminated well only when the sun struck them from the outside. If one wanted to see the entire glorious history of the Old and New Testaments recreated in the stained glass, one had to return again and again. To see the Battle of Jericho, one came just after dawn on a sunny day. That was the only time that scene on the northeast end of the church could easily be witnessed. To see David slaying Goliath, one came shortly after noon.

The nearby cathedral of Notre Dame was older—Pope Alexander II laid the cornerstone in 1163. Similar in its early Gothic style to the cathedral in Noyon it, too, had a west entrance framed by square towers. But it was much more massive with great flying buttresses, and its towers soared over two hundred feet high. Above the three portals at the main entrance stood twenty-eight kings painted in vivid yellows, blues, and reds. These were not kings of France but kings of Judea and Israel. The privileged could ascend the steps of the north tower, then cross the cathedral roof and continue to ascend in the south tower. The south tower was topped by a bell loft dominated by a thirteen-ton bell called "Emmanuel." Three enormous rose windows of red and blue glass dominated the inside of the cathedral.

It seems to me that things most grand and most colossal

are associated either with the king or with the church, reflected John.

The north side of the Seine River—called the "right bank"—where John lived was the commercial side of Paris. The other side of the Seine—the "left bank"—was considered the intellectual side because all the schools were south of the Île de la Cité. Over sixty colleges of various kinds existed, dominated by the complex of colleges constituting the University of Paris. Students in the University of Paris system numbered over twenty thousand. Faculty exceeded one thousand. The university was very powerful in French life, and it was dominated by the theologians of the Sorbonne who were staunchly loyal to the church of Rome.

To qualify for the study of theology, medicine, or law, all students—all over Europe—had to master the arts, which consisted of seven disciplines. The first three to be studied were the trivium: grammar, logic, and rhetoric. The next four—the quadrivium—were arithmetic, geometry, music, and astronomy. These seven arts survived from antiquity. But by the Middle Ages, they were enmeshed in elements of Catholicism throughout Europe. The seven arts were personified on the facade at the great cathedral of Notre Dame on the Île de la Cité. Grammar was an old crone with the rod of correction, Logic held the serpent of wisdom, Rhetoric clutched tablets of the poet, Arithmetic counted on fingers, Geometry flaunted compasses, Music pealed a bell with a hammer, and Astronomy displayed a primitive sextant.

But authorities deemed John Calvin not quite ready to enter even the Trivium. For a while, even though he had already studied *Donatus,* he studied Latin with a tutor, often with the d'Hangest boys. For they were now in Paris, also, although they lived in their own quarters. After John had polished his Latin, he was allowed to enter the Collège de la Marche in the lowest class, the fourth class. There he struggled with grammatical irregularities and anomalies, as well as with syntax and prosody. The textbook was the "Doctrinale" of Alexander of Ville-Dieu, with which students like John had struggled for the preceding three hundred years.

But then John was monumentally blessed. Mathurin Cordier began to instruct the fourth class. Years later, John reminisced with Cordier over what happened at the Collège de la Marche:

> *God's goodness gave you to me for a little while as preceptor, to teach me the true way to learn so that I might continue with greater profit. When you had charge of the first class (and what success you had!), you were faced with a troublesome problem. You saw that boys taught very ambitiously by other masters nevertheless lacked a solid foundation and had nothing but show, so that you had to start with them from scratch. You grew tired of it, and for that year descended to the fourth class. Well, such was your purpose, but for me this happy start to the study of Latin happened by the special blessing of God. I enjoyed your teaching only for a little space, since we were soon moved up by that stupid man who directed our studies according to his will, or rather his whim.*

*Yet I was so helped by you that whatever progress
I have since made I gladly ascribe to you. . . .*[1]

Cordier—latinized as "Corderius"—was a man of about
forty. He had introduced a unique way of studying Latin. He
intended to make the language live in the mind of the student, rather than try to fill the student's mind with mechani-
cal details. So he taught them how *not* to speak Latin! His
examples were all somehow wrong and had to be corrected.
Not only did his examples use that unique approach but his
examples all illustrated Christian morality.

One example after correction said:

> The good child loves the school,
> Virtue and God, and His Word;
> To the vicious all is displeasing
> That is pleasing to God.[2]

Another read:

> The good child tries to live,
> According to Jesus and to follow Him;
> The naughty child follows Antichrist
> And makes war on Jesus Christ.[3]

John learned hundreds of these examples from Cordier.
In the process of correcting them, he acquired Latin that
was pure and elegant. For Cordier was a purist who purged
Latin of all the foreign influences and sloppy extraneous
additions of the centuries. John knew Cordier was brilliant,

but of course he could not have known Cordier's book of grammar—*Colloquiorum Centuria Selecta*—based on his method would be used for the next several hundred years!

But grammar was just one subject. John also studied elementary logic, by means of a summation of Aristotle's *Organon*. This he and the other students learned by heart. Some boys understood it, some did not. A bright one like John mastered it. In addition, they learned some Latin poetry, mainly classical poetry like that of Virgil and Ovid. The students also studied arithmetic. The completion of de la Marche trained a youth to at least write letters in the formal language of Latin, or, as in John's case, to advance in school. John's progress was so rapid that in 1522 he was able to move on to the Collège of Montaigue to pursue a more rigorous mastery of the seven arts.

But he was not in a vacuum. Paris was alive with both rumors and truths. Exploration of the oceans was proceeding at a stunning pace. The Columbus voyages to distant isles in the west were old news. A vast continent in the west had been confirmed by yet other explorers. Even more remarkable was the voyage of Spain's Ferdinand Magellan. His expedition sailed completely around the world, confirming once and for all that the world was a sphere. Magellan was killed on the voyage, however, and only one of his ships survived the voyage, arriving in Spain in 1522. Of his original crews totaling 239 men, only 17 returned! Nevertheless Spain, Portugal, and even England were conquering the seas. And where was France? The French kings in their ignorance had opted out of these astonishing explorations. So it was no surprise that the French tended to belittle oceanic explorations.

In 1522, it seemed the notorious monk Martin Luther had not been murdered. He reappeared in Wittenberg. Apparently Frederick the Wise had been hiding him at one of his castles. In Wittenberg, Luther and his colleagues disbanded the local Augustinian cloister. Cloisters of monks and nuns, it was rumored, were dissolving all over central Germany. Apparently Emperor Charles V did nothing to stop it. It seemed this Martin Luther had truly broken a chunk of Europe away from the church of Rome. It seemed he was starting some new radical religion. Was it Christianity? He was widely regarded as a heretic by Catholics. But educated Catholics were not so sure. In France people were reading Luther's writings in Latin. The few who knew German read Luther's tract in German called *On Indulgences and Grace.* They were cautious about his conclusions but not his writing. His German was vigorous and imaginative. Readers had never read German that powerful.

"This angry monk may not only break with Rome but help forge a strong German nation out of all those princely domains," worried the French.

And what was happening in France? John found it hard to believe the preposterous stories he heard about King Francis I and his court. But alert young students—like John—shuttling back and forth from classes on the left bank to lodging on the right bank occasionally saw the king. He was young, turning only twenty-eight in 1522, with a wispy beard and mustache. He was married to Claud, the daughter of his predecessor Louis XII, and they already had five children. He was tall for the sixteenth century at six feet and broad shouldered. It was a good thing he was physically large because he swaggered about in furs, elegant fabrics, precious metals, and jewels. But not even all that could detract from his nose of epic proportions.

Francis I didn't like the palace at the Louvre on the right bank. It was gloomy, he said. He often resided in splendor at the palace on the Île de la Cité. He also frequented the palace called Les Tournelles by the Bastille, north of the Seine. He was often at the Fontainebleau, a hunting lodge in a lush forest south of Paris—a resort that he expanded into palatial proportions. There, masters of the hunt kept one hundred dogs and three hundred falcons at the king's disposal. Occasionally, the king was at a great chateau in Blois or other interesting localities. If the king was on the move it was impossible not to notice. His entourage was enormous.

Questioned about his extravagance, Francis I was said to have answered, "For such is our pleasure."[4]

Virtually at his elbows most of the time during non-public moments were his master of the household, his chamberlain, and four gentlemen of the bedchamber, also called first lords- in- waiting. Serving the gentlemen of the bedchamber were several dozen lords of the bedchamber, twelve pages of the bedchamber, and four ushers of the bedchamber. At the king's table, twenty lords served as stewards of his cuisine and managed a staff of forty-five men and twenty-five cup-bearers. Intermingled in this army of servants were dozens of pages and secretaries.

In his court were a cardinal who was grand chaplain of the royal chapel and a bishop who was master of the prayer service. Many others—clerics, scholars, poets, and such who served at the king's "pleasure"—were allowed to attend as grooms of the chamber. In the background were fourteen physicians and surgeons, four barbers, and numerous singers and musicians. Of course his wife, Claud, his mother, Louise of Savoy, and his sister, Marguerite, attended, too. They each had their own entourage: up to fifteen ladies-in-waiting and sixteen maids of honor. Each of the king's children also was surrounded by stewards, chancellors, tutors, pages, and servants. In the colossal kitchen were four chefs, six assistant chefs, and numerous cooks specializing in meats, soups, sauces, and pastries. Hundreds manned the king's stables and assisted him in hunting. Last but not least were four hundred well-trained archers in bright, colorful uniforms—the king's bodyguard.

So King Francis I did not move about Paris unnoticed!

He made a great show of collecting the finest art. He was going to make sure France participated in the Renaissance. This apparent open-mindedness to the arts disarmed the intellectuals who might have given him trouble. Rumors persisted that he spent a great amount of time wooing women, married or not. He made sure plenty of ladies worthy of his attention were always in attendance at court.

He explained gallantly, "A court without women is a year without spring and a spring without roses."[5]

But what did King Francis I accomplish for France?

In his mind the king's duty was to expand, to control. So naturally he involved himself in intrigues with and against the pope as well as with and against the emperor. They, after all, were of like minds and his chief rivals. The territory of Lombardy had flared up again. Francis I had placed two brothers of one of his favorite mistresses, the countess of Chateaubriand, in charge there. Sensing their weakness, the emperor Charles V was pressing for advantage. On the other hand, Francis I had sent French soldiers across the Pyrenees into Spain to try to take the territory of Navarre. The French were soundly defeated there. "Would there be an all-out war?" wondered Parisians. Could the king take his mind off art and women long enough to manage a war? He had recently made an enemy of the duke of Bourbon, the most powerful nobleman in France. The duke had advanced the king a fortune in the campaign to take Lombardy in 1515. The king would not repay the duke. To make matters worse, by 1521 the king and his scheming mother, Louise, were claiming the estate of the duke's dead wife!

Parisians sighed and spread the rumor that before Louis XII died he had grumbled of his successor Francis, "All our work is useless; this great boy will spoil everything."[6]

Yet Parisians shrugged. The intellectuals were thrilled that King Francis I seemed intent on making Paris the artistic center of Europe. After all, they congratulated themselves, Paris was already the intellectual center of Europe. The darling of all European intellectuals—the Dutch humanist Erasmus—had been educated there and now floated from one royal court to another. But his brand of humanism remained in Paris to take root. The humanism of Erasmus was not like the "secular humanism" of later centuries. Erasmus was a believer. So were his followers. His philosophy was so close to that of the Reformers like

Luther that many of them considered him an ally. What Erasmus did with his fluent Latin was to go back to the church fathers, those Christian sages of the first six centuries. He did not blindly accept the later teachings of the Catholic Church, the works of the so-called Scholastics. In so doing, Erasmus realized the necessity of reading the Bible in its original languages. To do that he had to learn Hebrew and Greek. So that's what he did. Paris intellectuals were still entranced with the possibilities. So was Martin Luther in Germany.

By 1516, Erasmus had published the New Testament with the "original" Greek and his Latin translation of the Greek side by side. His preface read:

> *I would have those words translated into all languages, so that not only Scots and Irishmen, but Turks and Saracens might read them. I long for the plowboy to sing them to himself as he follows the plow, the weaver to hum them to the tune of his shuttle, the traveler to beguile with them the dullness of his journey. . . Other studies we may regret having undertaken, but happy is the man upon whom death comes when he is engaged in these. These sacred words give you the very image of Christ speaking, healing, dying, rising again, and make Him so present, that were He before your very eyes you would not more truly see Him.*[7]

That certainly planted the seed. Yes, why not translate

the Bible into all the common tongues? Erasmus soon discovered the church of Rome had no intention of allowing such a thing. In fact, he and his writings were under scrutiny. Nevertheless, he had the courage to condemn certain church practices in print:

> *There are priests now in vast numbers, enormous herds of them, seculars and regulars, and it is notorious that very few of them are chaste. The great proportion fall into lust and incest and open profligacy. It would surely be better if those who cannot be continent should be allowed lawful wives of their own, and so escape this foul and miserable pollution.*[8]

How did Erasmus escape the wrath of the church of Rome whereas Luther could not? The main reason was that Luther was a monk; Erasmus was a secular scholar. Also, Luther was defiant, Erasmus was conciliatory. Luther was ferocious, Erasmus was retiring. In any event, Erasmus did not dare reside in a Catholic stronghold like France. But the writings of Erasmus inspired many scholars and nobles in France to question the church and its writings.

It seemed to John and his friends that scholars all over Paris were now inquiring into such matters. One of the most notable in 1522 was sixty-seven-year-old Jacques Lefèvre d'Étaples, also called "Faber Stapulensis." From his scholarship, Lefèvre had published two tracts asserting that Mary, sister of Lazarus, Mary Magdalene, and the woman who anointed Christ's feet in Luke 7:37 were three distinct persons. For this seemingly mild assertion, which differed from the teaching of the church of Rome, Lefèvre drew a barrage of criticism. Coupled with the outrage was Lefèvre's commentary on the Epistles of Paul published in 1512. Close scrutiny showed that many of his conclusions preceded the same conclusions of Martin Luther! Lefèvre postulated that Christians can be saved only by faith in the grace of God, not by good works. Lefèvre, like Luther, urged a return to the gospel. Lefèvre was condemned by the theologians of the Sorbonne. He was attacked by the leading official in John's Collège of Montaigue, Noel Bedier. Wisely, Lefèvre withdrew from the fray to live quietly in Meaux, not far east of Paris.

His former pupil Guillaume Brigonnet had been bishop of Meaux since 1516. Brigonnet was very sympathetic to reform. He appointed benefices to such known reformers. Reformers as Lefèvre, William Farel, Louis de Berquin, Gerard Roussel, and Francois Vatable. To illustrate just how complex the intellectual environment was in France, Marguerite—the sister of King Francis I—applauded Brigonnet's efforts. But as the Sorbonne zealots became more and more vocal in their condemnation of the reformers, Brigonnet lost courage. Like Erasmus, he considered the unity of the church more important than reform. Nevertheless, in 1523, Lefèvre published the New Testament in French and was translating the Psalms into French. The Sorbonne now called him a heretic. But Marguerite's sympathies toward scholars like Lefèvre shielded them, at least temporarily.

No one in France could stop the flow of Luther's ideas

41

from the east, either. Students and merchants imported writings of the ferocious monk. Luther's writings from Germany were eagerly discussed as the most exciting news of the day. More than nobility, teachers, students, and scholars weighed the ideas of the German reformer. Luther even inflamed merchants and tradesmen. He seemed to have the answers for all wrongs, and he supported his answers with passages from the Bible.

Some of the tradesmen, inspired by the German reformer, became zealots themselves. A wool-carder in Meaux called the pope the Antichrist. A mob branded him on the forehead as a heretic. But a much worse incident occurred in Paris, and John Calvin probably witnessed it.

four

In August 1523, the French Parliament reviewed the charge against an Augustinian monk, Jean Valliere, that he conspired with the Reformers. To his sympathizers, he had done nothing more than read some of Luther's works in Latin and then talk about them. But the nobility noted Luther had also been an Augustinian monk. And the nobility wanted to send a warning that France would not have its own Luther. So the Parliament sentenced Jean Valliere to death. Criers trumpeted the execution throughout Paris. It would be hard to imagine that John Calvin and the other students did not witness this spectacle. With much fanfare, executioners led the monk to the great square in front of the cathedral of Notre Dame. There he stood, far removed from the Mass inside. Then they led him to the pig market outside the city walls. No witness to his execution could ever erase the gruesome memory.

"His tongue was ripped out," a witness gasped. "Then he was tied to a stake and burned."

Cynics noted that whereas Princess Marguerite protected intellectuals, she despised monks and priests. Nevertheless, France was becoming very dangerous for intellectual dissenters like Lefèvre, too. John Calvin probably never worried about Lefèvre, but he certainly must have worried about his own relative from Noyon, Pierre Robert. Pierre was nicknamed Olivetan, because he "burned the midnight oil." He was only three years older than John. He was already inflamed by the ideas of Erasmus and Lefèvre. He longed to translate the original Hebrew and Greek of the Bible into everyday French. So he feverishly prepared himself. But, though John heard these things in 1523, at the age of fourteen he was in no position to do anything but continue his own studies. And speaking of these things around his own school of Montaigue was unwise. Noel Bedier was a very surly watchdog for the church of Rome.

"He would light the fire under your feet," John's friends warned grimly.

Situated among many schools on the left bank, the Collège of Montaigue was about one-half mile south of the great cathedral of Notre Dame. Forty years before John arrived, Montaigue had been reformed by its principal, Jean Standonck. Erasmus himself had attended the school nearly thirty years before. Erasmus had few good words for Standonck:

In this college there then reigned Jean

44

*Standonck, a man with no evil feelings, but entirely
deprived of judgment. Indeed, in memory of his
youth, which he spent in the most extreme poverty,
he concerned himself with the poor, and this should
be strongly approved. And if he had relieved the
misery of young men enough to furnish them with
what was necessary for hard study, but without per-
mitting excessive abundance to disorder them, this
would have merited praise. But that he attempted to
achieve this by giving them a bed so hard, a diet so
strict and so little abundant, vigils and labors so
overpowering that in less than a year from beginning the experiment he had brought numerous
young people, gifted by nature and highly promis-
ing, either to death, or blindness, or madness, or
even sometimes to leprosy (I knew several of them
personally), so that he clearly put every one of
them in danger; who would not understand that
this was cruelty to those around him?[1]*

But many, perhaps better able to endure hardship better
than the irritable Erasmus, considered Standonck an able
educator. As in so many cases of enlightened educators,
Standonck himself had been schooled in the evangelical
mysticism of the Brethren of the Common Life. He was
imbued with the spirit and aims of its founder, Gerard
Groote. The unselfish devotion of the brethren was known
all over the Catholic world because one of Groote's pupils,
Thomas of Kempis, wrote a classic devotional book called
The Imitation of Christ. Standonck had aspired to make

Montaigue into a fine religious college to prepare priests and monks. Pupils recited the daily offices of the church and observed the great feasts of the church.

Whereas most Parisian schools allowed their students to drink and carouse, Montaigue strictly regimented its students. Montaigue expected students—just as if they were in religious orders—to self-examine their behavior at all times and make regular public confession of sins. Montaigue encouraged students to denounce others who sinned. Years later, stories surfaced that John Calvin was nicknamed the "Accuser" at Montaigue because he excelled at denunciation. However, all stories arising from the Catholic community later about Calvin, as well as Luther, are suspect.

Like all the other students at Montaigue, John arose at four o'clock for the morning office or specified prayers, next a lecture, then Mass. About seven o'clock he ate a very meager breakfast, and then until eleven o'clock he attended the main lectures and discussions. Then came the main meal of the day. Compared to the cuisine at the home of the Montmors in Noyon, John's food at school was pig swill. Bread was dry and coarse. In addition they received a pat of butter, a bit of fruit, and cheese or herring. Their drink was watered-down wine. Students who were not registered for theology received even less. One of the few good things about the meals was that bread was not rationed. A student could at least get his fill. Also, the meal was accompanied by readings from the Bible or about the life of a saint. School announcements and a prayer concluded the main meal.

Various activities occupied students until three o'clock

when the real classes resumed. At five, they had vespers. From five to their bedtime at eight o'clock they had another small meal, and participated in discussions. Two days a week they had free time. For someone like John with uncle Richard or his wealthy friends from Noyon nearby, use of this free time was never a problem. Theology students received extra privileges at the school, but there existed yet another division within the students. The richest students ate at the school at a common table but lodged at homes in the neighborhood. The poorest students lived at the college and had to perform menial chores for the college. Montaigue segregated the poor from the rich both in chapel and in the classroom. Montaigue trusted the rich to maintain their own hygiene; the school regularly inspected the poor for lice and fleas. John Calvin numbered among the rich students. Ironically, it seemed only Pierre Tempete, the enforcer of discipline at Montaigue, treated everyone equally.

"He whips all students, rich or poor," grumbled his victims.

It is known that John at first studied under a preceptor who was Spanish. Possibly, but not certainly, the Spaniard was the terminist philosopher Antonio Coronel, who taught at the school at the time. Terminism was an extreme form of nominalism, one of three schools of philosophy—the other two being Scholasticism and humanism—struggling for dominance in John's day. The monk Thomas Aquinas in the thirteenth century had championed the old classical philosophy of Aristotle. For over two hundred years, religious scholars had built on that philosophy, which came to be known as Scholasticism. The church and most universities still espoused Scholasticism in the 1520s. But in the fourteenth century, William of Occam had introduced a severe kind of empirical philosophy called nominalism. Nominalism allowed for nothing abstract. Though William of Occam hesitated to use his approach to attack beliefs in God and the church, his later followers did not. If they couldn't see a phenomenon with their own eyes, then it did not exist. Nominalists—also called empiricists or realists—asserted God could not be proven to exist. Neither nominalism nor humanism had official acceptance in the church-dominated Paris schools in the 1520s.

Yet it is quite possible John Calvin fell under the influence of an extreme nominalist at Montaigue, though school officials closely watched teachers in those days. Antonio Coronel may have been a terminist, but he could not have been dogmatic. Lectures were invariably commentaries on specific books in the curriculum. The teacher had a choice of two forms of presentation. One was a straightforward explanation or exposition of the text. The teacher dealt with the smallest details, forbidden by regulations to skip any material. The second method of presenting material was in the form of extracting from the book the most important problems and arguing for and against them. The extraction in itself was subject to the teacher's interpretation. Nevertheless, this was a widely used method and one the student could expect to use throughout his life. In essence, he had to publicly defend a given thesis or set of theses in opposition to a master. The student had to defend his arguments with syllogisms. Syllogisms were the tools of logic—mathematical in nature—first known to be developed by Aristotle. In their simplest form, they are two short two-term premises and one short two-term conclusion. For example, the disputants agree on two premises: "All French people live under the king" and "People in Noyon are French people." Then the conclusion is "People in Noyon live under the king." The disputants must agree the conclusion is true, or disqualify one of the premises as false. More complicated syllogisms were developed, as well. The method became a fundamental form of argument in John's time. The key was of course to validate the premises.

"False premises can be used to promote false conclusions," the teachers cautioned.

The faculty integrated this kind of disputation into the oral tests for degrees, which took place in the schools during the winter months. The faculty presented the student with sets of theses to defend on the subjects he had studied. The source material was dominated by Aristotle, with contributions from Euclid, Ptolemy, Boethius, Pierre d'Ailly, and John Pecham. Only d'Ailly on geography and Pecham on optics were not writers from classical antiquity. To adequately defend these subjects, the student had to have mastered syllogistic argument. In fact, the more advanced students honed their skills by lecturing. If they were unable to defend their presentation against the arguments of their young listeners, they were hardly ready to take on the masters.

In addition to this rigorous formalized study, it is probable John Calvin read many of the same things Luther had read earlier at the University of Erfurt in Germany. John read the works of Priscian, the best-known Latin grammarian,

Petrus Hispanus (Pope John XXI), and Thomas Aquinas. He surely also read more of the Romans Ovid and Virgil. Virgil's fame as the greatest Latin poet rested on his epic *Aeneid*. But the church world read him for another work, his *Eclogue*. Although Virgil wrote the fourth of the ten eclogues forty years before the birth of Christ, his work was interpreted as Messianic. In elevated poetry, it prophesied the birth of a child who would bring back the golden age, banish sin, and restore peace. A few skeptics huffed in private that Virgil had really meant a child expected from the union of Marc Antony and his wife, Octavia, sister of Augustus.

"But even granted that," reasoned John, "Virgil's work is an excellent example of a work that had a second, greater meaning."

The precocious John Calvin of Noyon fulfilled all the requirements for his master of arts degree in the winter of 1525–1526. Most masters were at least twenty-one. John was sixteen. And that winter King Francis I was in a terrible mess. In spite of his interests in art and lavish living, Francis I sparred constantly with the emperor Charles V. The embittered duke of Bourbon had gone over to the emperor's side in 1523. Egged on, Francis I sent an army after him, commanded by Bonnivet, the beau of his sister, Marguerite. Bonnivet was not only incompetent but a coward, fleeing his command. The French army suffered terrible losses. Then Francis I really began to worry. It was rumored the duke of Bourbon was plotting with both the emperor and England's King Henry VIII to attack France from three sides! But only the duke attacked. This time France routed their adversary. The duke fled into Italy.

Francis I was emboldened. His wife, Claud, had died and he had no taste for mourning. He decided it was time to storm into Italy and take Naples away from the emperor. But he first had to conquer Pavia, then Milan. Only thirty, Francis I himself led the siege. But the city of Pavia held off the French for four months. Each day Pavia weakened, but so did the French army. In the meantime, the duke of Bourbon and Italian allies raised an army of twenty-seven thousand. On February 24, 1525, the duke's enormous army on one side, as well as angry soldiers sallying forth from Pavia on the other side, attacked the French forces. The French, so sure of victory only the day before, panicked. The king, suffering many wounds, was captured.

Francis I was imprisoned in a fortress near Cremona, east of Milan and Pavia. From there he sent a dismal message to his mother, Louise:

> *Madame, that you may know how stands the rest of my misfortune: there is nothing in the world left to me but honor and my life, which is saved. And in order that in your adversity this news might bring you some little comfort, I prayed for permission to write you this letter. . . entreating you, in the exercise of your accustomed prudence, to do nothing rash, for I have hope, after all, that God will not forsake me. . . .*[2]

What a predicament for a French king!

Francis I had no choice but to humble himself before the emperor. He wrote to Charles V, "if it please you to

51

have so much honorable pity as to answer for the safety which a captive king of France deserves to find. . . you may be sure of obtaining an acquisition instead of a useless prisoner, and of making a king of France your slave forever."[3]

Charles V responded with his terms for peace and the liberation of King Francis I. His terms made it very obvious there had been a secret pact among himself, the duke of Bourbon, and King Henry VIII of England. They all were to receive compensation. To satisfy the emperor, France must give up all claims to Burgundy, Flanders, Artois, and Italy. To satisfy the duke of Bourbon, France must give up all claims to properties inherited by his wife. To satisfy Henry VIII, France must give England a great portion of northern France. In addition, Francis must join the emperor in his campaign against the Turks.

"The demands are staggering, mountainous!" gasped the court of Francis I.

The king's mother, Louise, the ruling monarch in his absence, refused. She began to raise an army. She sent envoys to urge the Turks to attack the emperor. She began to negotiate with the pope, Clement VII. Did the pope really want the emperor to become so powerful? She asked Henry VIII of England the same question. In the summer of 1525 Henry VIII wavered and, instead of demanding northern France, accepted millions in gold from France to sign an alliance with them. Shocked by the shrewd Louise's ability to sway opinion, Charles V moved Francis I to a castle in Spain, near Madrid.

There Francis I became very sick. Charles knew a dead king was worth nothing. He became more receptive to negotiation. He allowed Princess Marguerite to visit her brother in September. Still, Charles, even without England, held out for the rest of his terms. In January 1526, the worn-down Francis signed with Charles the Treaty of Madrid. To make sure Francis honored the terms of the treaty after he was freed, the emperor would hold the king's two oldest sons. To make matters even more distasteful to Francis, the emperor insisted the king marry his sister, Eleonora, Queen-Dowager of Portugal! There was no encumbrance on Francis I because his wife, Claud, had died. So Francis I married Eleonora, and, leaving his sons Francis and Henry imprisoned, he returned to France in late winter of 1526 with his new bride Eleonora.

"I am a king again!" the shameless monarch roared.[4]

Who could have imagined such an improbable adventure?

But Germany was having its own adventure, all too probable and all too tragic. As usual, it had been the brilliant Luther who had seen it coming. As early as 1521, when he was himself a fugitive from the emperor, he published *An Earnest Exhortation for All Christians, Warning Them Against Insurrection and Rebellion.* Luther saw very well that radical reform of religion would also encourage lawlessness in many oppressed people who had grievances. He wrote:

> *It seems probable that there is danger of an uprising. . . For the common man has been brooding over the injury he has suffered in property, in body, and in soul, and has become provoked. They have tried him too far, and have most unscrupulously burdened him beyond measure.*

> *He is neither able nor willing to endure it longer,*
> *and could indeed have good reason to lay about*
> *him with flails and cudgels, as the peasants are*
> *threatening to do. . . .*[5]

Later, Thomas Muntzer had approached Luther in Wittenberg. Muntzer claimed motivation not from Holy Scriptures but from an inner knowledge given him by the Holy Spirit. Luther wanted nothing to do with him. Luther kept warning of the danger:

> *Insurrection is unreasoning, and generally*
> *hurts the innocent more than the guilty. Hence no*
> *insurrection is ever right, no matter how good the*
> *cause in whose interest it is made. The harm result-*
> *ing from it always exceeds the amount of reforma-*
> *tion accomplished. . . . When "Sir Mob" breaks*
> *loose he cannot tell the wicked from the godly; he*
> *strikes at random, and then horrible injustice is*
> *inevitable. . . . My sympathies are and always will*
> *be with those against whom insurrection is made.*[6]

Thomas Muntzer, meanwhile, had taken root in the Saxon town of Allstedt. There he established a zealous church. His followers destroyed all images. They prohibited infant baptism. They touted dreams as a way to communicate with God. Owning land was wrong. It belonged to everyone. So did property. Muntzer railed against all opposition. He enlisted many peasants into his movement. Luther knew something about movements. Muntzer was hatching an armed rebellion. Luther warned his patron, Frederick the Wise.

Frederick summoned Muntzer to meet with him and Luther. Muntzer saw this as a threat and fled to another jurisdiction. There he began to build his rebellion again, ranting that Luther was the "Wittenberg pope." By the fall of 1524, Muntzer and Hans Muller organized peasants in southern Germany under "Twelve Articles" in an "Evangelical Brotherhood." Essentially the brotherhood refused to pay taxes, church tithes, and feudal dues. They wanted rights to hunt, fish, and cut wood in the forests. These privileges were very appealing to peasants. By the spring of 1525, the movement had spread throughout the south and was reaching north to Frederick the Wise's Saxony. Naturally the peasants—numbering in the tens of thousands—wanted to know where Luther stood. Probably many had been recruited with the promise that Luther would deliver their demands.

By April 1525, Luther had written a treatise titled *An Exhortation to Peace on the Twelve Articles of the Swabian Peasants*. He tried to summarize arguments on both sides: peasants and nobility. But he also admonished both sides. Luther rarely pulled a punch. An excerpt aimed at the clergy and nobility read:

> *We need thank no one on earth for this foolish rebellion but you, my lords, and especially you blind bishops, parsons and monks, for you, even yet hardened, cease not to rage against the holy gospel, although you know that our cause is right, and you cannot controvert it. Besides this, in civil*

*government you do nothing but oppress and tax to
maintain your pomp and pride, until the poor
common man neither can nor will bear it any
longer. The sword is at your throat, and yet you
still think you sit so firm in the saddle that no one
can hoist you out. You will find out that by such
hardened presumption you will break your necks. . .
If these peasants don't do it, others will; God will
appoint others, for He intends to smite you and will
smite you. . . .[7]*

But Luther also turned his pen on the peasants:

*It is my friendly and fraternal prayer, dearest
brothers, to be very careful what you do. Believe
not all spirits and preachers. Those who take the
sword shall perish by the sword and every soul
should be subject to the powers that be, in fear
and honor. If the government is bad and intolera-
ble, that is no excuse for riot and insurrection, for
to punish evil belongs not to every one, but to the
civil authority which bears the sword. Suffering
tyranny is a cross given by God. . . .[8]*

Luther went on to insist that even if the Twelve Articles
were all just, the peasants had no right to implement them
through by force. He finished the treatise with a plea for
peace. But it was too late. On April 16, bands of rebellious
peasants had stormed Weinsberg and massacred many. In
the next two weeks they burned monasteries and castles to

the ground. The once very able Frederick the Wise was deathly sick. The rest of the nobility seemed paralyzed by the uprising. Luther was sickened by the violence rendered by the peasants. Rapes and murders were unconscionable. In Franconia alone 270 castles and 52 cloisters were demolished. The Palatinate had completely fallen. It really looked as if Saxony would fall, in fact, all of the German-speaking world. At that point Luther found himself rallying the civil authorities to restore order and guarantee peace for its citizens. The peasants felt betrayed, although Luther had always preached against insurrection.

In May, the conflict came to a head at Frankenhausen where the peasants assembled an army of eight thousand. Against them, Philip of Hesse led an army of equal size but better trained and better armed. But Philip had already come to terms with his own peasants and was inclined to grant new liberties to attain peace. He convinced the peasant army to negotiate. All might have ended in justice had not Thomas Muntzer arrived from Mulhausen. He craved total victory and incited the peasants to battle. The peasants responded. They were routed. Thousands died.

"Muntzer has been executed!" trumpeted the news through Europe.

In 1526, Europe was in a colossal upheaval, and France seemed in the hands of a moron. Unbelievably, Francis I—ever active, ever optimistic—now entered into an alliance called the League of Cognac with Pope Clement VII and the Italian provinces. The emperor's reaction—other than raging at the king's captive sons—was not against France. Emperor Charles V decided the pope must be punished. An imperial army of German and Spanish troops poured down into Italy and sacked Rome, killing four thousand Romans in the skirmish. The invaders imprisoned the pope in the Castle San Angelo, east of the Vatican palaces. It seemed young Emperor Charles V, who had not quite known how to handle the ferocious Luther in 1521, had found his voice by 1526.

"And where is my ally France?" worried the pope.

Francis I sent an army into Italy under the leadership of Lautrec. Lautrec struck everywhere but Rome. Finally even the Italians turned on him. Lautrec died and his French army disintegrated. The emperor had clearly vanquished everyone. He demanded reparations from Francis I. But haughty Francis I and the angry emperor could no longer communicate civilly. Once again it was the king's mother, Louise, now fifty, who was the voice of calm and reason. She negotiated with the emperor's forty-six-year-old aunt, Margaret of Austria, regent of the Netherlands. Francis I, for the return of his sons, would abandon all claims to Flanders, Artois, and Italy. He would also pay the emperor two million gold crowns. But he was allowed to keep Burgundy. The claims of the duke of Bourbon were no longer an issue. He had died in those Italian wars of 1526. The two princes of France returned to their lives of luxury, but the royal fiascoes—would insanity be a better word?—continued. To oppose the emperor, Francis I began negotiating an alliance with Henry VIII of England, the German princes, the pope, and the Turks!

It was in this milieu of craziness that John Calvin began his study of law in 1526.

five

Yes, John Calvin was to study law.

John's father, Gerard, had decided John should become not a priest but a lawyer. John later wrote:

> *Ever since I was a child, my father had*
> *intended me for theology; but thereafter inasmuch*
> *as he considered that the study of the law com-*
> *monly enriched those who followed it, this expec-*
> *tation made him incontinently change his mind.*
> *That is the reason why I was withdrawn from the*
> *study of philosophy and put to the study of the*
> *law, to which I strove to devote myself faithfully*
> *in obedience to my father.*[1]

The reason for his father's decision was sound enough,

but another reason was undoubtedly unstated. The influence and the protection that the Calvins enjoyed from the church in Noyon were unraveling. Charles d'Hangest was no longer the bishop of Noyon. He had managed to pass the important position on to one of many nephews, Jean d'Hangest. But Jean was immature, often not in residence. The chapter of elders at last had clearly gained the upper hand. They were making demands. Gerard was executor of the many chaplaincy accounts. He had been given a deadline of Saint Remy's Day—October 1—of that year to give a full accounting. Whether because of poor record-keeping, incompetence, or dishonesty, he was not going to be able to give a full accounting.

But Father is not the only Calvin who will be held accountable, thought John.

John had failed to observe some technicalities regarding his benefice. As a chaplain he was supposed to attend full chapter meetings. To get a waiver from these meetings, he was required to get the rector of the university to write that John was a student at the university. But he had become slack about that technicality. For many years the chapter had ignored that oversight, probably because of the protecting influence of the bishop of Noyon. But not now in 1526. The situation had changed. He had not been condemned yet but labeled difficult, obstinate, intractable.

"Officially I am 'contumacious,' " he told his friends.

Somehow Gerard learned of the brilliance of Pierre de l'Estoile at Orléans, some sixty miles south of Paris, and that is where John Calvin went to study law. Orléans was a country village compared to Paris. The town was along the north side of the broad, shallow Loire River. The town of broad boulevards had the very large Cathéedrale of Sainte-Croix, but the church offered nothing unique after Paris. The fame of Orléans rested on its outstanding school of law and the memory of the Maid of Orléans. The town, once of much greater importance and heavily fortified behind towered and gated walls, had been under siege by the English for seven months in 1429. It was not ancient history to John or the inhabitants of Orléans. It had happened less than a century before John Calvin arrived.

"Yet it seems quite miraculous," he mused.

Joan of Arc, not even a woman but a girl of sixteen, told the French nobles that God had willed her to defeat the English invaders. The French were desperate enough to try anything. As Joan approached Orléans with her entourage of soldiers, the town authorities sallied forth in another direction to create a diversion. So in spite of many surrounding English strongholds, Joan entered the town with her reinforcements. The town fathers urged caution. They would not attack the English until real reinforcements arrived. Joan waited impatiently several days, but suddenly one evening she heard voices and screamed, "The blood of France is being spilled!"[2]

Inspired, she rushed forth with her force of several hundred soldiers and began toppling one English stronghold after another. Within a few days she had conquered every stronghold, including the greatest one—Les Tourelles—on the south side of the river at Orléans. Her only blunder—if one could call mercy a blunder—was to allow most of the English forces to escape. Later for revenge they would kill

61

her. All over Orléans there were memories of Joan of Arc. Of course she had visited the cathedral. But she had also crossed the great medieval bridge across the river. She had stayed at the fine home of Jacques Boucher, too.

Well, where had she not been in such a confined place? wondered John Calvin, who had lived in the immensity of Paris.

John had entered a new world in many ways. Although the university in Orléans had been founded in 1305, it did not practice the harsh discipline of the Paris schools. It was no coincidence that two of the d'Hangest boys were there, also. John lodged at the house of the lawyer Nicolas Duchemin on the rue du Pommier. John did not hide the degree of warmth he felt for his friends. He may have looked cool and reserved, but for his studies and his friends he was passionate. In a 1532 letter to the considerably older Nicolas Duchemin he wrote:

> *Whatever happens, I shall see you again.*
> *Remember me to Francois Daniel. . .and your*
> *entire household. . .Adieu, dear Duchemin, my*
> *friend dearer to me than my life.*[3]

So John was quite happy in Orléans and spoiled, too. As Theodore Beza—who lived in Orléans himself at the same time—would write later:

> *Some persons, still alive, who were then on*
> *familiar terms with him, say, that, at that period,*
> *his custom was, after supping very frugally, to*

> *continue his studies until midnight, and on getting*
> *up in the morning, to spend some time meditating,*
> *and, as it were, digesting what he had read in bed,*
> *and that while so engaged, he was very unwilling*
> *to be interrupted. By these prolonged vigils he no*
> *doubt acquired solid learning, and an excellent*
> *memory. . . .[4]*

John now enjoyed a well-balanced scholastic and social life. He developed dear friends besides his old friend Claude d'Hangest and his new friend Nicolas. One friend was Francois de Connan, fellow law student and son of a government official in Paris. Philip Lore was a bookseller of the town, so there was little doubt he was soon well acquainted with John the bookworm. Perhaps the friend who helped John the most socially was another law student, Francois Daniel. Francois was a native of Orléans. Once again John was virtually taken into another family as a son and a brother.

John Calvin's earliest preserved letters are from and to these friends in Orléans. It is only beginning with this period of time that future historians were able to move beyond a murky figure of history to document a real personality. Even at that, complicating any future attributions was John's fondness for pseudonyms, a playful partiality he would retain for life. Sometimes he wrote as Charles d'Espeville, Espeville, or Eppeville, those names reflecting a village from which his chaplaincy of La Gesine drew support. Yet he also used the name Passelius, a village not in his chaplaincy but belonging in the realm of the d'Hangests. He also wrote under a scrambled version of his name.

"Martinus Lucanius," he noted with satisfaction.

Orléans had no collegiate system. Although the master who kept a student hostel disciplined students, he did it for social propriety, not for saving young souls. There was only one faculty, that of Law, consisting of five professors of Civil Law and three professors of Canon Law. Although the faculty was not as rigorously Catholic as the colleges in Paris, it was not secular, either. Some of the professors were clerics in holy orders. Many—professors and students— wore the tonsure.

John became a student of Civil Law. Law as his world knew it stemmed from the Romans. In the reign of Justinian, between 529 and 534, all previous Roman law and legal writings were arranged and modernized into the *Corpus JIuris Civilis*. The *Corpus JIuris Civilis* was refined throughout the Middle Ages. It consisted of three parts—the Codex, the Digesta, and the Institutiones—of which the Codex was the core. The Codex was the definitive statement of Roman law. The Digesta was a massive historical compilation of Roman jurists, which resulted in the Codex. The Institutiones was a condensed but authoritative version of the Codex that was used as a textbook for students. John was struck by the usefulness of the Institutiones.

What a great idea, he reflected.

John was lectured on the Codex and selected portions of the Digesta. He, as well the other students, was expected to also study the Institutiones on his own. The greatest recent influence for John's study of Law was the fourteenth-century jurist Bartholus. His vast commentaries applied the dialectics or syllogistics that had also been applied to theology.

This then was roughly the Scholastic method in Law. But just as the Scholastic method was under attack in theology, so was the dialectic method in Law. Humanists—especially Valla, Politien, and Bude—were trying to reduce the importance of Roman law.

In a sense, this was calculated to remove religion from the Law. For the Codex was full of religious elements. Parts of the Codex dealt with church law in Rome, church buildings, bishops, baptism, heretics, images—even the doctrine of the Trinity. But the humanists had not yet diminished the Codex in Orléans. If John had not done so before, at Orléans he surely gained a thorough knowledge of church doctrine and its history as well as Christology. This latter was specifically the study of the nature of Christ. Christology was quite extensive in that Christ was first revealed in the prophecies of the Old Testament, then unfolded in the historical reality of the New Testament.

It could be argued that I've received my most rigorous theological training not in Paris but in Orléans*!* he cogitated.

Yet John also studied the down-to-earth application of the Law. How did the Law handle marriage, divorce, inheritance, water rights, property rights, leases, disputes between neighbors, and dozens of other human problems? John seemed to have a special talent for rationalizing such problems. After John received his bachelor's degree in Law he was allowed to lecture. These lectures were usually on the Institutiones. However, in John's case, he actually was allowed to fill in for professors on key lectures on the Codex and Digesta. Theodore Beza recorded that "in a little while he was regarded, not as scholar, but as one of the docteurs ordinaires, and he was more often teacher than hearer."[5] John was definitely one of the most highly regarded students at Orléans.

John admired Pierre de l'Estoile, who was reputed to be the best French jurist of the time. Although l'Estoile was staunchly traditional Catholic in his faith, he was open-minded in his treatment of most other opinions. If a humanistic opinion survived logical dispute, then he would use it in his juridical science. Pierre de l'Estoile was a priest who had entered the orders after the death of his wife. In John's own words, he was struck by "his penetrative mind, his skill, his experience in law, of which he is the unchallenged prince of our epoch."[6] His only rival in France was Andrea Alciati, the famous Italian Romanist at Bourges.

"If Pierre de l'Estoile has a flaw, it is his hostility toward the new evangelicals of Luther," said John and his friends.

Just how far had John come from the "old-fashioned" Scholastic training at Montaigue? It seems—from his statement later that he was "obstinately addicted to the superstitions of the Papacy"[7] at the time—that in Orléans he might have resisted the evangelicalism of Luther, even humanism. But another of his statements, that "the polemics of Luther against Zwingli and Oecolampadius concerning the Holy Communion"[8] dissuaded him from reading those two, indicates he was quite impressed with Luther. By 1526, Luther had published such intriguing treatises as *On Civil Government, On the Order of Worship, The German Mass,* and *On the Enslaved Will.*

On the other hand, some of John's acquaintances were known to be friendly with Sucquet, a protégé of the most highly esteemed humanist of all, Erasmus. Erasmus had been critical of the church but remained loyal, so openly admiring Erasmus was not nearly as dangerous as openly admiring Luther. Most of the humanists had little interest in the Reformation. They were elitists, more interested in languages and literature than the dogma of the church in Rome. This aloofness may well have been John's attitude.

"Until I met Wolmar at Orléans," he would remember later.

Melchior Wolmar, a German from Rothweil, maintained a boarding school for boys, one of whom was young Theodore Beza. Although thirteen years older than John, Wolmar was a peer in his studies. Wolmar's formal education proceeded so slowly because he had taken up the study of Greek. He had already published an annotated edition of two books of the *Iliad*. Unsaid was the tantalizing fact that the New Testament was originally written in Greek. At some time in Orléans, Wolmar began to teach John Greek. In the future, John would refer to Wolmar as "my particular friend."[9] Wolmar was also a committed Reformer! Many would later speculate it was Wolmar who first began to convince John that Luther's evangelicalism was firmly based on the New Testament.

John's relative Pierre Robert, known as Olivetan, also lived in Orléans. Olivetan, a very committed evangelical, was not as discreet as Wolmar. He had already been forced to flee Paris. He still burned with the ambition to translate the Bible into everyday French. Surely young John Calvin, now in a much freer environment, must have frequently talked to Olivetan. Many were excited by Luther's 1522 translation of the New Testament from Greek into German. People in Orléans like Melchior Wolmar who knew German as their native tongue insisted Luther's New Testament was monumentally important. Luther had learned Greek under two very fine Greek scholars, Philip Melanchthon and George Lang. Although Luther wrote in the court German of Saxony, his diction was so elevated, so powerful, so moving it seemed to outsiders he had created a new version of German.

"Luther's German is staggering," enthused Wolmar.

Olivetan could scarcely wait to accomplish something similar in French. But even Orléans was not completely free of authorities who sought out dissidents. By 1528, Olivetan was forced to flee Orléans for Strasbourg on the Rhine River. Strasbourg was by then a stronghold of evangelicals. Olivetan took refuge with the leading Reformer there, Martin Bucer. After Luther and his protégé Melanchthon, the thirty-seven-year-old Bucer was the most widely respected evangelical in Europe. Bucer was a mediator, always trying to reconcile the differing positions of Luther and Zwingli and others among the Reformers. The protection and freedom of Strasbourg was a great stroke of fortune for Olivetan. John Calvin, nineteen years old in 1528, knew of all these intrigues.

Who is right in all this theological conflict? he agonized.

In 1529, John surrendered his benefice at the cathedral of Noyon to his younger brother, Antoine. In 1527, he had received outside the Noyon chapter the benefice as curate of

Saint-Martin de Marteville in the Vermandois. In 1529, he was able to exchange this benefice for the one at Pont l'Évêque, the hometown of his grandfather. That was arranged by none other than his old friend Claude d'Hangest, who by then was the abbot of St. Eloi. Then John's life took a sudden turn. In 1529 Melchior Wolmar left for Bourges. And in that very same year John followed him there.

Bourges was even smaller than Orléans. But it was a stately town, built atop a hill where the Yèvre and Auron Rivers joined and within miles flowed into the Cher River. Bourges was very ancient, having been a town worthy of siege by none other than Julius Caesar in 52 B.C. Kings had favored it in the century before John arrived. Charles VII had lived there fifteen years. Louis XI had been born there. The great champion for Charles VII, Joan of Arc, had wintered there one year. Bourges had been ravaged by a fire in 1487. As a result—except for the great stone Cathedral of Saint Etienne and the Palace of Jacques Coeur—the town seemed fresh and new.

Dominating the hill was the cathedral, yet another built in the Gothic style. This cathedral, as many in France, had superb stained glass windows, but it also had some unique touches. There were no chapels built off the side at the east end near the altar. Somehow this made the nave seem even higher. And the side aisles were as high as any John had ever seen. For the first time in his life, John expressed a particular desire.

"It seems a glorious ambition to speak in such a great church," he admitted.

But to the residents of Bourges, what distinguished

their town was that it was under the wing of the king's sister, Marguerite—since her marriage in 1527, known as Marguerite of Navarre. Marguerite was now a lady of thirty-seven, not a beauty—with a long-nosed face like her brother's—but a famed charmer. Fables said "she was born smiling, and held out her little hand to each comer."[10] Two years older than Francis I, she had been his "little mother." She was devoted to him. The fact that she was so fond of him contributed to his popularity, because the people of France adored Marguerite. In truly caring for poor people Marguerite was exceptional for royalty. She actually visited poor people in their hovels, and sent them food and medical help from her court. She called herself the "Prime Minister of the Poor."[11]

Marguerite was pious but independent of church discipline. Moreover, she considered the rank and file clergy hypocrites and rakes. She was not popular with the very hard-core Catholic clergy and scholars in Paris. Nevertheless, she was open to both Catholicism and the new evangelicalism. She particularly liked mysticism. She agonized over truth and wrestled with doubts. Was God cruel? Was Scripture really God's words? Her spiritual struggle was very much like that of John Calvin and his friends.

Marguerite was an intellectual, rare among the royalty. She had learned Spanish, Italian, Latin, Greek, and some Hebrew. She was kind, offering sanctuary to those who had offended authorities: scholars, poets, philosophers—even theologians. When Louis de Berquin was arrested for translating some of Luther's works in 1523, it was Marguerite who convinced the king to free him. She allowed dissidents into her court. She collected hundreds of stories from these inquisitive, controversial people. She could certainly hold her own with them. She was a prolific writer, but only the privileged knew she was one of the best poets of the time.

"I left Orléans for Bourges because of Marguerite," admitted Melchior Wolmar.

Marguerite knew Wolmar's evangelical fervor was getting some unwelcome attention in Orléans, so she encouraged Wolmar to come to Bourges. He would be safer there. This triggered the move of John and several of his friends, among them his fellow law student, Francois Daniel. As a university Bourges had struggled. Founded as recently as the 1460s by King Louis XI, it had been bitterly opposed by academics in both Paris and Orléans. From the first day, the University of Bourges had not only offered the *Corpus JIuris Civilis* with its three parts—the Codex, the Digesta, and the Institutiones—but also the additional Authentica. The Authentica was little more than a justification of absolute monarchy. But by the fifteen hundreds, even the kings lost interest in Bourges and its university. The university probably would have perished except for a fortunate political development. In 1517, Francis I gave the duchy of Berry to his sister Marguerite. The duchy included Bourges. She not only sheltered dissidents but invigorated the university at Orléans by attracting well-known, high-powered professors.

"Fortunately for us, she got Andreas Alciati, the only professor of Law who can rival Pierre de l'Estoile," said John and the other law students from Orléans.

Alciati was considered almost revolutionary in juridical science. Essentially, he promised law based on humanism, in contrast to Pierre de l'Estoile who offered law based on Scholasticism. Alciati had the reputation of taking law far beyond dry, arbitrary detail. Reputedly he was capable of expressing law by great general principles, and of illuminating law by history and literature. In other words, Alciati had supposedly honed law into a science. This promise of cutting-edge law lured students from all quarters. Surely Alciati's reputation appealed to a meticulous logician like John Calvin.

But Alciati regarded the French—including l'Estoile— as barbarians. He snorted that surely the students "preferred teaching to fantasies, clarity to uncertainty, elegance to obscurity, Latin to barbarism. . . ."[12]

John Calvin's opinions of Alciati became mixed. He was impressed by his humanism. He was pleased with Alciati's elegant use of Latin. But John did not like his arrogance. More than that he was disturbed by his breeziness. John considered Alciati quick and overconfident to the point of being sloppy in contrast to the plodding but meticulous l'Estoile. Alciati's personal attacks on l'Estoile particularly displeased John. To John, these emotional indulgences were inexcusable in the arena of ideas. Yet, apparently l'Estoile had attacked Alciati in a pamphlet. And Alciati had responded in kind. Ironically, John found himself helping his friend Nicolas Duchemin prepare a pamphlet titled "Antapologia." It was an attack on Alciati. But Nicolas tired of the project. Then, remarkably, John alone was preparing the pamphlet for printing.

The truth was that although John was ostensibly a student of law at the university—soon to receive his degree in law—he was involved in numerous activities, ever more dissenting. First of all, John continued to study Greek under Wolmar. This was daring. This pursuit was condemned by the church. An earlier cleric at Orléans had warned, "We are finding now a new language called [Greek]. We must avoid it at all costs, for this language gives birth to heresies. Especially beware of the New Testament in Greek; it is a book full of thorns and prickles."[13] Yet John and his friends pursued Greek vigorously. Their icons, of course, were the great humanist Erasmus and the Reformer Luther, both of whom had fearlessly plunged into the original Greek of the New Testament.

John would later deem the study of Greek under Wolmar "one of the most important things that happened to me."[14]

But now John truly circulated among the most powerful people in France. For he had met Marguerite of Navarre. And only the king and his mother, Louise, were more powerful contacts than Marguerite of Navarre. At twenty-one in 1530, John felt the complete scholar. He could tackle any subject: French, Greek, or Latin. Perhaps he had developed a sympathy for evangelicalism, but it was hidden. In the vein of a classicist like Erasmus, he began writing a commentary on Seneca's *De Clementia*.

six

De Clementia was written in Latin by the famous
Roman and Stoic philosopher Seneca, who was
a contemporary of Jesus. Seneca was also advi-
sor to the notoriously cruel Emperor Nero. It was Nero
who eventually had Paul and Peter martyred in Rome. *De
Clementia*—or "On Mercy"—was an appeal by Seneca to
Nero to be magnanimous and show mercy. Why did John
pick this particular work? Was it in the hope that King
Francis I would read it and show mercy to the growing
number of Reformers? Was John ready to become a
Reformer himself? Or did he select *De Clementia* because
he saw an underlying Christian-like sentiment in Seneca's
stoicism? Or did he choose it because it gave him a chance
to show up the most recent analysis of the work done by
none other than the esteemed Erasmus? No one can be

sure. But he certainly did not pick the work to show its parallel with biblical principles. He mentions the Bible only three times and each time in a very offhand way. Perhaps John Calvin did it to establish himself as the new Erasmus on the scene. Erasmus had himself been only partly satisfied with his commentary and actually invited his readers to do better. John eagerly took the challenge.

Surely the great Erasmus himself will read my commentary, John must have thought with pleasure.

In one passage of his commentary, John seemed full of his own importance:

> *I think, however, that I have now brought the work so far that if anyone more learned, more felicitous, and with more time at his disposal, shall improve upon this edition. . . Seneca will, I have every hope, be read with a minimum of trouble and a maximum of pleasure. . . [however,] I would like to see this author explained with notes, like little stars, to exclude the temerity of those who would corrupt the text.*[1]

John wrote a lengthy work in Latin, considering *De Clementia* itself was a work of only about fifteen thousand words in Latin. He dedicated the work to Claude d'Hangest. John followed that with a biography of Seneca. Then John examined the text of *De Clementia* with his own notes on each passage. His lawyer's training showed in that he repeatedly presented the "facts," then argued the meaning. His analysis was mainly philosophical and philological, the latter being an inquiry into the exact meanings of words themselves. But he used other methods, as well, including explanatory and historical. John quoted no fewer than fifty-six Latin classical writers, twenty-two Greek classical writers, numerous humanists of his own time, and only seven church fathers.

"Yet I appealed to one Father of the Church, Augustine, no less than fifteen times," he noted with some surprise.

John Calvin and his contemporary scholars admired Seneca and the classical writers in general. Certainly Seneca's appeal to Nero for mercy was a noble thing. Seneca and the Stoics agreed with Christians in affirming the existence of a supernatural providence. On the other hand, Stoics attributed importance to man as man, much in harmony with basic beliefs of the humanists. Lastly, the Stoics loved truth and scientific research, characteristics humanists also revered. But though John admired the classical writers, he by no means spared Seneca. Stoicism's pride in showing no emotion too often just masked insensitivity. Apathy and the lack of pity were not to be admired.

> *We should be fully persuaded that pity also is*
> *a virtue; that a man cannot be good if he is not*
> *merciful, whatever may be argued by these sages,*
> *idle in their ignorance; I know not whether they*
> *be wise, as Pliny would say, in any case these are*
> *not men. It is of the nature of man to feel pain, to*
> *be moved by it, to resist it nevertheless, and to*
> *accept consolations, but never to have no need*
> *of them.*[2]

John insisted it was a necessary part of being human to grieve, to laugh, to shed tears, to feel. Stoicism isolated a person. Following individual conscience did not necessarily result in caring for neighbors. Stoicism fell far short of Christianity. So, as admirable as *De Clementia* was for its time, it was insufficient for John.

"I have reasoned that the use of Stoicism can not even lead to reliable conclusions," he marveled.

Thus, John at twenty-one toiled on the work. He had very high hopes for it. This was the state of John's development in 1530—apparently a budding humanist—although he was still intrigued by the writings of Luther. His erudition on so many subjects made him a popular guest speaker, and not only in university circles. He spoke on rhetoric at the Augustinian convent where a future Reformer, Augustin Marlorat, was prior. Moreover he also preached in local churches. It is known he preached at Asnieres and at Linieres. One of his listeners, Philbert de Beaujeu, recorded with faint praise that at least John Calvin was telling his listeners something new. But whatever John told them was not considered heretical in any way. John was still regarded a "good Catholic."

Yet John struggled with his trust in the church of Rome. Objectivity was difficult because, by 1531, the Calvin family in Noyon was immersed in difficulties with the church. Gerard was virtually disgraced. John's brother Charles was outraged at their fall from grace. Anger consumed him. Was he also a heavy drinker? John feared he would soon do something rash to lose his chaplaincy. How did this turmoil at Noyon influence John? It certainly must have relieved him of any worry about how his own defection from the church might embarrass his family. For, at some unrecorded time at Bourges, John changed from a humanist Catholic like Erasmus into a humanist evangelical! He alluded to his conversion vaguely in his later writings:

> *God drew me from obscure and lowly begin-*
> *nings and conferred on me that most honorable*
> *office of herald and minister of the gospel. . .*
> *I tried my best to work hard [at law], yet God*
> *at last turned my course in another direction by*
> *the secret rein of His providence. What happened*
> *first was that by an unexpected conversion He*
> *tamed. . . a mind too stubborn for its years—for*
> *I was so strongly devoted to the superstitions of*
> *the Papacy that nothing less could draw me from*
> *such depths of mire. And so this mere taste of true*
> *godliness that I received set me on fire with such*
> *a desire to progress that I pursued the rest of my*
> *studies more coolly, although I did not give them*
> *up altogether. Before a year had slipped by, any-*
> *body who longed for a purer doctrine kept on*
> *coming to learn from me, [although I was] still*
> *a beginner, a raw recruit. . . .[3]*

Yes, while at Bourges, to his own surprise John fell in with the evangelicals. He flamed with a desire for righteousness. One ancient observer recorded that while at Bourges John Calvin spoke in a "barn." This was precisely the kind of thing dissidents did. Yet, events in Noyon abruptly interrupted John's rich experience at Bourges. He learned in early 1531 his broken father, Gerard, was seriously ill in Noyon. In March, on the way home, he stopped in Paris to arrange the printing of Duchemin's pamphlet "Antapologia," written against Alciati. John took credit only for writing the preface.

"There, friend Duchemin's work is delivered," he said with satisfaction and continued on to Noyon.

Although John had always obeyed his father, he did not exhibit a profound love for him. Perhaps his father had been too ambitious for him. His father had virtually sent him away from the house at a very tender age. If anyone had raised him it had been the d'Hangests. Claude d'Hangest was more of a brother to John than Charles Calvin. So John did not take Gerard's final illness as hard as one might expect for a son. Besides, Gerard was seventy, old for sixteenth-century France. Moreover, he was doted on by his second wife, a woman John knew no better than a social acquaintance.

John was also distracted. He and his brothers had to try to get his father a plot in consecrated ground. The chapter was being difficult. Funerals were quick in those days, and there was little time to quibble. But the truth was that his brother Charles was no help at all. In February, Charles had vented his anger against a messenger from the chapter. He assaulted him. Two days later Charles assaulted a cleric. At least those were the official accusations of the chapter. So Charles was very close to being excommunicated. He certainly was no help to John and Antoine in finding a burial place for their father. Once again John had to depend on the influence of the d'Hangests. And once again they helped him.

John wrote Nicolas Duchemin on May 14:

> *When I left you, I promised to return soon, and I have been worried that I could not do as I wished. When I was thinking of returning, my father's illness kept me back. The physicians gave us hope of his recovery to complete health; and this only made my longing to see you grow sharper after a few days. But day after day has passed, and we have now reached the point where no hope is left; he cannot recover. But whatever the outcome, I will come and see you. . . .*[4]

Was John going back to Orléans or Bourges? "But why go to either place?" he reasoned. He had taken law as far as he wanted. There was a new course of study that had been initiated in Paris. The king—probably persuaded by sister Marguerite—had liberalized what could be openly taught. His readers were called the "King's Readers." They were actually lecturing on Greek and even Hebrew. Besides that opportunity in Paris, John had been inspired while arranging the printing of Duchemin's pamphlet to get his own study on Seneca printed. That was practical only in Paris. So when John's father finally died in late May and John had seen him buried in sacred ground, he headed not to Bourges or Orléans but to Paris. And the King's Readers.

"I will seek lodging near the lectures of Pierre Danes, protégé of the noted humanist and classicist Bude," he decided.

Several socially prominent families offered John lodging. John was a desired guest. He was not only erudite but tactful. He was also known as a problem solver. No sooner had he settled in Paris than the Daniel family in Orléans had him arrange for their daughter to enter a convent in Paris. John, discreet and cautious, spoke to the girl first. She assured him she was enthusiastic about entering a religious order. So in June 1531, he arranged the entry into the convent, accompanied on his mission by Nicolas Cop.

Cop's father was a personal physician to King Francis I. Although only four years John's senior, Nicolas Cop was already a very high official in the university system. John at twenty-two had many older influential friends. This was possible because of his advanced maturity and his reputation for intellectual prowess. It also may have been possible because he now circulated in a network of those sympathetic to the new evangelicalism. Nicolas Cop was such a sympathizer. Initially, these people were drawn into the network because they could vent their frustrations with the abuses and malpractices of the Catholic Church. But as they discussed Luther's ideas, more and more of them agreed with Luther's challenge of Catholic beliefs. Cop was intrigued by all of Luther's ideas. Yet he remained, like Erasmus, loyal to the church of Rome. In 1531, Cop's changing beliefs were known only to his friends.

In early 1532, John supervised in Paris the printing of his Commentary on *De Clementia*. He explained the situation to his friend Francois Daniel in a letter dated April 22:

Well, at length the die is cast. My Commentaries

on the Books of Seneca, De Clementia, *have been printed, but at my own expense, and have drawn from me more money than you can well suppose. At present, I am using every endeavor to collect some of it back. I have stirred up some of the professors of this city to make use of them in lecturing. In the University of Bourges I have induced a friend to do this from the pulpit by a public lecture. You can also help me not a little, if you will not take it amiss; you will do so on the score of our old friendship; especially as, without any damage to your reputation, you may do me this service, which will also tend perhaps to the public good. Should you determine to oblige me by this benefit, I will send you a hundred copies, or as many as you please. Meanwhile, accept this copy for yourself, while you are not to suppose that by your acceptance of it, I hold you engaged to do what I ask. It is my wish that all may be free and unconstrained between us. Adieu, and let me soon hear from you. . . .[5]*

So even though he could barely afford the effort, John ambitiously proceeded. He did not hesitate to ask friends to promote the book. "Would you mind mentioning the book in your lectures?" he asked various friends at the universities in Paris, Orléans, and Bourges. "Would you mind ordering one hundred copies?" he asked his bookseller friend, Philip Lore. John so vigorously promoted the book, one would have to conclude that he had little interest in pursuing law, and that he very much wanted the life of a classical scholar like Erasmus.

In a letter he joked that unless Duchemin offered him a bed, he would have to "freeze under the open sky."[6]

For in the next months, he moved about among Orléans, Paris, and probably Bourges. He even attended the chapter in Noyon. Scholars politely discussed John's Commentary on *De Clementia*. They certainly did not hail it as a masterpiece. Did the cool reception to his book among scholars steer him even more in the direction of the evangelicals? His exact motivation at this time is not known. However, by early summer of 1533, John Calvin seems to have taken that particular direction in earnest. This is indirectly evident in the sophistication and depth of knowledge he would display in his writings about evangelical Christianity only two years later. But his relationship with Nicolas Cop at the time furnished direct evidence.

On November 1, 1533, Cop gave his inaugural address as the new rector of the University of Paris. John had helped him draft the speech. The subject was the Beatitudes, the profound words of Jesus recorded in the fifth chapter of the Book of Matthew. John and Cop had borrowed much from Erasmus. They had been influenced much by Luther. Cop began his remarks with a plea worthy of Erasmus for purifying Christianity through a study of the Bible in its original languages. Then he expounded on *salvation through grace and faith,* a theology worthy of Luther. Cop concluded his speech with an appeal for tolerance of the new evangelical reformers. What did his friends think of his speech?

"Run for your life, Nicolas!" they warned.

Cop's speech had set off an explosion. Not just the

theologians but also the nobility called for Cop's head! His life was in peril. There was the terrible possibility he would be executed. Or murdered because a reward for Cop had been announced of three hundred gold crowns—dead or alive! Cop fled to Basel in Switzerland. Basel was not only the home of Erasmus but home to many evangelicals. Powerful friends warned John to be very careful. Then he heard his room at the Collège of Fortet had been searched and all his papers confiscated. In John's room was a copy of Nicolas Cop's speech in John's own handwriting. That would surely make some conclude he had written the speech himself! John not only never went back to the Collège of Fortet but avoided Paris completely. Nevertheless he was reluctant to leave France. He wasn't as notorious yet as Cop. Perhaps the authorities weren't even looking for him. However, at one point when he sought asylum with Marguerite, she told him bluntly he would be safer somewhere else. No amount of optimism could overcome that gloomy wisdom from Marguerite.

I may be a little fish, John concluded, *but I am considered a heretical little fish.*

Incredibly, John was relieved. He had been shamed by keeping his beliefs secret. It was cowardly. Cop had felt the same way, which led to his speech. They would not be like "Nicodemites," believers at night but non-believers in the day. They would not be oppressed by fear. But France was dangerous for John, and he would be wise to remain inconspicuous. John sought refuge with Louis du Tillet, a friend from the earliest student days in Paris. Louis had three brothers, all influential in government and the church. Louis himself was a curate of the village of Claix and a canon in the local cathedral of Angoulêeme. Louis sheltered John at the family estate at Claix. John was delighted. The personal library of the du Tillets consisted of several thousand volumes. One could find all of Luther and Zwingli, as well as all the church fathers like John's favorite, Augustine.

"The library is a small paradise for a scholar," he mused.

But John still ventured forth. In May he was in Noyon to resign his two benefices. He would no longer be a hypocrite. Except for his refuge at Claix he kept on the move. Records show his presence at Noyon, at Orléans, at Poitiers. If he slipped into Paris, there is no record. John met other dissidents, of course. He met Anabaptists, notorious since the Peasant War in Germany. He wrestled with some of their unique ideas. Was infant baptism wrong? At death did the soul "go to sleep," only to awaken at Judgment Day? He even wrote a treatise titled "Psychopannychia" or "Upon the Sleep of Souls." Through Scriptures he concluded that the soul was instantly with Christ. What a contrast this treatise was from his secular treatise on Seneca. Now he relied almost entirely on Scriptures. However, he was unable to have "Psychopannychia" published in France.

"The printers are watched very carefully now for dissident material," warned powerful friends.

Marguerite was cautious but consistent in her support of dissent. But Francis I had a history of what seemed like vacillating. In fact, he usually responded to political situations. If the pope was getting too close to the emperor, Francis I would shake him up by relaxing restrictions on the dissidents. To please the pope, Francis I would act in the other direction. Sometimes Francis I wanted to please German princes. In that case he eased up on the dissidents. So the situation was always in flux. Francis, in most situations, would tolerate scholarship. But open defiance was another matter altogether.

"Cop went too far," grumbled the king's court.

Yet, in late 1534, there arose in France a faction of evangelicals who were far more radical than Cop and his friends. The timing of the uprising was unfortunate because Francis I—whatever his true motives—was actually negotiating with Luther in an attempt to reconcile German evangelicalism with French Catholicism. Francis I had invited Melanchthon, Luther's right-hand man, to come to France and "confer with some of our most distinguished doctors as to the means of re-establishing in the Church that sublime harmony which is the chief of all my desires."[7]

Suddenly, in October 1534, dissidents posted placards all over France. The messages on the placards were inflammatory. They declared the Mass was idolatry. The pope and the Catholic clergy were "vermin. . . apostates, wolves. . . liars, blasphemers, murderers of souls."[8] Cautious evangelicals were horrified by this excessive display. But much worse, the vandals even managed to get a placard on the king's bed-chamber at Amboise. Francis I exploded. His agents arrested dissidents everywhere. Two hundred were arrested by the middle of November. Through the next three months twenty were officially executed. The king's agents also encouraged mobs to assault reformers. In January 1535, mobs in Paris burned six protesters to death. In February, Etienne de la Forge, one of John's own Parisian friends, was burned to death. By the month of May, mobs in Paris had burned to death a total of twenty-four. Luther heard of these atrocities. All negotiations ended with Francis I. Besides, it was rumored, Luther thought the French reformers were weak, not true evangelicals anyway.

Where was John Calvin?

He wisely had fled France on horseback in October. His destination was Basel, where friend Cop was well established. John was accompanied by Louis du Tillet, who had compromised himself by befriending many dissidents, and du Tillet's two servants. Their overnight stop at Metz on the German border was disastrous. One of the servants realized that neither John nor du Tillet wanted to backtrack into France. So in the night he stole their money and fled on one of the horses back to France. The thief was correct in believing they would not follow. They had to rely on the tiny amount of money the other servant had. The three men were fortunate to reach Strasbourg, where they stayed with none other than Martin Bucer. John had exchanged letters with the Reformer. And of course Bucer knew John's relative Pierre Robert, or Olivetan, very well.

"However, Olivetan has moved on to Basel," Bucer informed John.

From Strasbourg the three refugees continued on to Basel, arriving there in January 1535. The town set upon the south bank of the Rhine River. An earthquake had savaged Basel in 1356. The result was that even the structures in the town that survived the trembler had been rebuilt in strong Gothic style. Like all European towns of any worth, Basel had protective walls with several city gates. The word "gate" did not do justice to these massive entrances. John went through just such a gate—the "Spalentor"—on the north side of Basel. Twin thick-walled towers enclosed a complicated and very deadly system of barriers. The towers were cylindrical, of course, so those inside had a clear view of the outside of the town wall. There was nowhere for an unwelcome intruder to hide in the age of cannons and even primitive muskets that exuded projectiles from the loopholes in the towers.

To actually enter the city, one trudged through a series of barriers within the gate that had to be raised. John shuddered, knowing unwanted entrants could be trapped between two barriers. There, they were at the mercy of "murder holes" in the stone archway of the gate over their heads. A dozen excruciating ways of killing men lurked behind those holes, including boiling oil. Because of the armament and murderous supplies that had to be stored in the gate complex, a peaked tower was built above the archway. But the murder holes were just an option. There were trapdoors, too, in the great entrance. One could suddenly plunge into a pit of spikes! While passing through one of these terrible gates, John liked to suspend his imagination.

"Yet within this murderous gate, Basel welcomes dissidents like myself," reflected John Calvin.

seven

Basel had a great cathedral, a thriving university, and many churches. Oecolampadius, friend of Zwingli and Erasmus, had led Basel to evangelicalism. In 1531, when Zwingli was killed in the Battle of Kappel, Oecolampadius, only forty-nine, was said to have lost the will to live and died. How John would have relished talking to Oecolampadius, who just six years before at the Colloquy of Marburg had debated the great Luther. Yes, John was at last in the realm of the Reformers. Yet the town harbored humanists like Erasmus, as well. John found company among Sebastian Munster, Heinrich Bullinger, and William Farel. Best of all, he was reunited with his dear friend Nicolas Cop and his relative Pierre Robert—or Olivetan. Because Basel bordered France and the German provinces, both languages were spoken. But German predominated.

However, intellectuals like John were at home anywhere in Europe because all spoke Latin. According to his later colleague and confidant Theodore Beza, John lodged with Simon Grynaeus and Wolfgang Capito, both advanced students of Hebrew. John undoubtedly met Erasmus. But the meeting could not have been a lively one. Erasmus at seventy-one was in fading health.

Worried confidants correctly prophesied, "Friend Erasmus has only one year to live."

John's past studies served him well. Olivetan immediately enlisted him in his own project: a long-needed French translation of the Bible. Waldensian Christians had commissioned the work in 1532. Olivetan intended to have it printed in the summer of 1535. Olivetan was an accomplished student of Hebrew. He had personally translated the Hebrew of the Old Testament into French. However, his Greek was shaky. Olivetan had cobbled together a translation of the New Testament. He revised Lefèvre's New Testament in French by sometimes translating from the Greek original, sometimes translating from the Latin edition of Erasmus. Olivetan asked John to review his translation of the New Testament in the time available—as well as write two prefaces, one in Latin and one in French. Then Olivetan left for Serrieres near Neuchâatel where he was going to have the Bible printed. Later that year John wrote a friend:

> *It seemed to me that I could put this task*
> [reviewing Olivetan's treatment of the New
> Testament] *off to do at my leisure. Meantime, I*

*gave myself to other studies and forgot about it—
or rather, languished in my usual laziness. At any
rate, I have not yet started on it. . . But from now
on I will take care to set aside an hour a day for
this work. . . .[1]*

Of course, "I gave myself to other studies" indicated
John was working on something else. And it was nothing
less than his magnum opus—the "great work"—of his life!
Yes, John Calvin in 1535 was already polishing final drafts
of the *Christianae Religionis Institutio* or the *Institutes of
the Christian Religion.* In the literature of law, the term
"Institutes" referred to a condensed but authoritative ver-
sion of the Codex that was used as a textbook for students.
"Institutes" was greatly appreciated by the law student
John Calvin.

*Now this is how I hope to advance the understanding
of Christianity,* John told himself.

To believe that he could have forged the first edition of
this great work in a few months in 1535, while he was also
helping Olivetan with his translation of the Bible, is naïve.
He must have been working on it for some time, probably
roughing it out for the first time back in the magnificent
library of the du Tillets. Surely at Claix John had digested the
powerful, brilliant writings of Martin Luther. There, John
was able to flesh out his understanding of Christianity—
inevitably in terms of the new evangelicalism. For he had
convinced himself the beliefs of evangelicalism were truer to
the teachings of Christ in the Bible than the beliefs of the current Catholic Church. Evangelicalism was even closer than

the current Catholic Church to the teachings of the early church fathers like Augustine.

John's actual acceptance of evangelicalism must have been even earlier. Perhaps he began seeing the need for his *Institutes* in Bourges as early as 1530 or so. Certainly he must have articulated Christianity in a very appealing, convincing way for intellectuals. For he later wrote of his student days that "anybody who longed for a purer doctrine kept on coming to learn from me, [although I was] still a beginner, a raw recruit."[2] Probably many of his friends had suggested how valuable his lucid explanations of Christianity would be for all those trying to understand Christianity.

But John wanted desperately to convince King Francis I, who was now persecuting all religious people who had abandoned the Catholic Church, that the new evangelicalism was true Christianity. Only the Erasmians—those with basic evangelical beliefs who nevertheless professed loyalty to Rome—were spared the wrath of Francis I. These included Brigonnet, Lefèvre, Roussel, and, of course, the king's own sister, Marguerite. But John and others could not compromise themselves. If only he could sway Francis I.

So John prefaced the *Institutes of the Christian Religion* with the "Epistle to Francis I." The preface ran many pages. Even the official title was quite lengthy: *The Basic Teaching of the Christian Religion comprising almost the whole sum of godliness and whatever it is necessary to know on the doctrine of salvation. A newly published work very well worth reading by all who are studious of godliness. A Preface to the most Christian King of France, offering to him this book as a confession of faith by the author, John Calvin of Noyon.*

In the preface John wrote to his monarch Francis I:

When I began this work, Sire, nothing was further from my thoughts than writing a book which would afterwards be presented to your Majesty. My intention was only to lay down some elementary principles, by which inquirers on the subject of religion might be instructed in the nature of true piety. . . But when I perceived that the fury of certain wicked men in your kingdom had grown to such a height as to leave no room in the land for sound doctrine, I thought I should be usefully employed if in the same work. . . I exhibited my confession to you, that you may know the nature of that doctrine which is the object of such unbounded rage in those madmen who are now disturbing the country with fire and sword. For I shall not be afraid to acknowledge that this treatise contains a summary of that very doctrine, which, according to their clamors, deserves to be punished with imprisonment, banishment, proscription, and flames, and to be exterminated from the face of the earth. I well know with what atrocious insinuations your ears have been filled by them, in order to tender our cause most odious in your esteem; but your clemency should lead you to consider that if accusation be accounted sufficient evidence of guilt, there will be an end to all innocence in words and actions. . . .

You yourself, Sire, can bear witness of the

false calumnies with which you hear it [our cause] daily traduced: that its only tendency is to wrest the scepters of kings out of their hands, to overturn all the tribunals. . . to subvert all order and government, to disturb the peace and tranquility of the people, to abrogate all laws, to scatter all properties and possessions and, in a word, to involve everything in total confusion. . . .

Wherefore I beseech you, Sire—and surely it is not an unreasonable request—to take upon yourself the entire cognizance of this cause, which has hitherto been confusedly and carelessly agitated, without any order of law, and with outrageous passion rather than judicial gravity. Think not that I am now meditating my own individual defense in order to effect a safe return to my native country; for though I feel the affection which every man ought to feel for it, yet, under the existing circumstances, I regret not my removal from it. But I plead the cause of all the godly, and consequently of Christ Himself. . . .

Is it probable that we are meditating the subversion of kingdoms?—we who were never heard to utter a factious word, whose lives were ever known to be peaceable and honest while we lived under your government, and who, even now in our exile, cease not to pray for all prosperity to attend yourself and Your kingdom!. . . Nor have we, by Divine Grace, profited so little in the Gospel, but that our life may be an example to our detractors

*of chastity, liberality, mercy, temperance, patience,
modesty, and every other virtue. . .*

*Though you are now averse and alienated
from us, and even inflamed against us, we despair
not of regaining your favor, if you will only read
with calmness and composure this our confession,
which we intend as our defense before Your
Majesty. But, on the contrary, if your ears are so
preoccupied with the whispers of the malevolent
as to leave no opportunity for the accused to speak
for themselves, and if those outrageous furies, with
your connivance, continue to persecute with impris-
onments, scourges, tortures, confiscations, and
flames, we shall indeed, like sheep destined for the
slaughter, be reduced to the greatest extremities. Yet
shall we in patience possess our souls, and wait for
the mighty hand of the Lord. . .for the deliverance
of the poor from their affliction, and for the punishment of their despisers, who now exult in such perfect security. May the Lord, the King of Kings,
establish your throne with righteousness and your
kingdom with equity. . . .*[3]

John's preface contained only a few of the invectives—
scathing rhetoric—so common of the period. It was meek
and mild compared to the stinging, slashing rhetoric of
Luther. It was the calm, logical development of a man
trained in law. He pleaded with the king to also take up their
case with "judicial gravity." The evangelicals did not ask
for mercy or toleration but for justice. Calmly, he reminded

the king that the official religion of the nation of France was Christianity. Patiently, he explained to the king that evangelicals, not the current church of Rome, represented the true beliefs of the early church. To prove his case, he would show that the evangelicals adhered to that most powerful statement of faith, the Niceno-Constantinopolitan Creed, often called just the Nicene Creed. The early church fathers had all agreed on the creed—expressed in Greek—at a great conference in A.D. 325. They reaffirmed the creed at Constantinople in A.D. 381, in the process clarifying the divinity of the Holy Spirit. The Nicene Creed read:

> *We believe in one God, the Father, the Almighty, maker of heaven and earth, of all that is seen and unseen. We believe in one Lord, Jesus Christ, the only Son of God, eternally begotten of the Father, God from God, Light from Light, true God from true God, begotten, not made, one in Being with the Father. Through Him all things were made. For us men and for our salvation He came down from heaven: by the power of the Holy Spirit He was born of the Virgin Mary, and became man. For our sake He was crucified under Pontius Pilate; He suffered, died, and was buried. On the third day He rose again in fulfillment of the Scriptures; He ascended into heaven and is seated at the right hand of the Father. He will come again in glory to judge the living and the dead, and His kingdom will have no end. We believe in the Holy Spirit, the Lord, the giver of life, who proceeds from the Father and*

*the Son. With the Father and the Son He is wor-
shipped and glorified. He has spoken through the
prophets. We believe in one holy catholic and apos-
tolic Church. We acknowledge one baptism for the
forgiveness of sins. We look for the resurrection of
the dead, and the life of the world to come. Amen.*[4]

All believers of the sixteenth century considered the
Nicene Creed inviolate. This then was the statement of fundamental beliefs John set out to confirm in evangelicals. If
not, John wrote the king, then indeed condemn us. Critics
had objected that the evangelicals were novel, they had no
stated doctrine, they attested to no miracles, they strayed
from true Christianity, and they splintered even among
themselves. All these criticisms of evangelicalism John
would address in his argument to the king. He could not
resist taking a jab at the Roman Church as he listed the criticism of evangelicals being novel: "I have no doubt our
teaching is novel to them. So is that of the Bible and of the
Church fathers."[5] In effect, John was declaring that the
church of Rome had strayed from the true Christianity of
the early fathers of the church.

John appealed to the king's love of his own French
people:

*All I had in mind was to hand on some
rudiments by which anyone who was touched
with an interest in religion might be formed to
true godliness. I labored at the task for our own
Frenchmen in particular, for I saw that many*

97

were hungering and thirsting after Christ and yet that only a very few had even the slightest knowledge of him. The book itself betrays that this was my purpose by its simple and primitive form of teaching. . . .[6]

In a sense, then, John was writing the *Institutes* for believers, too. Yes, those struggling in the faith. Yes, they were baptized but had since been overwhelmed by their sins. They were drowning, hanging on to what the early church father Jerome had called the plank of penance. They had a conviction of sin but worried constantly that they had not remembered every sin, confessed every sin. They had no peace. They went on pilgrimages. They fasted. They punished themselves. This was the very agony the young Martin Luther had inflicted upon himself for years. John wanted to instruct these poor souls struggling with the doctrines of the Catholic Church on how to reach true godliness with Christ and find peace.

After the preface to the king—logical and passionate though probably futile for such a politically motivated monarch—John constructed the *Institutes* on roughly the same outline as Martin Luther's "Small Catechism." The first three chapters explained the three fundamental authorities of Christian living: the Ten Commandments, the Creed, and the Lord's Prayer. The fourth chapter discussed which sacraments are truly biblical. But John's *Institutes* went beyond what Luther covered in his catechism. In John's chapter following the biblical sacraments, he took on the knotty problem of five sacraments that were not biblical. John's sixth chapter explained Christian liberty, church government, and civil government.

Chapter one, which dealt with the Ten Commandments, began with the profound sentence: "The sum of sacred doctrine is contained almost entirely in these two parts: the knowledge of God and of ourselves."[7] In other words, theology should not concern itself with God outside His association with man, nor with man outside his association with God. Once again, it was Luther who had persuaded John to base his theology on the belief that the ultimate and real truth about man is found only in the decisions and judgments of God. From man's viewpoint, God and man are inseparable. John repeatedly used the phrases "in the sight of God" and "with God." John developed his story of man and God in strict adherence to the Bible. Adam was a supreme man, granted wisdom and holiness, even immortality. But Adam sinned and lost the divine gifts. He became a man alien to God. All mankind since Adam carried that burden of ignorance, sinfulness, and mortality.

God delivered His commandments for righteousness again through Moses. So man knew what was required, yet because of his pride could rarely keep the Law. John insisted that the Mosaic Law was used to convince man of his lowly state, his hopelessness. Finally, God the Lawgiver entered into a union with man through His Son, the one man able to fulfill the Law. For fulfilling the Law, He was granted immortality. But Christ is so perfect, He shared His reward with man by paying the ransom for sinful man. Man to be saved, therefore, must only believe. No longer must he worry about whether his obedience to the Law has earned salvation.

Nevertheless the Christian must try to obey the Law. It is the way a Christian demonstrates that he both fears and loves God. The whole intent of the Law, said John, was to teach love. John explained each of the Ten Commandments in such a way that he could conclude how its observance demonstrated love for God. Yet he reminded his readers they must not fall back into the habit of living for the Law. Because that habit, without faith, led to uncertainty and anguish. Once again, the believer would be obsessed with remembering and confessing every sin.

This development of the commandments led naturally into the next chapter on faith. "For wavering, varying, being carried up and down, hesitating, living in suspense, losing all hope, these are not faith. Faith is an unshaken, sure, and completely certain determination of the mind; it is having somewhere to rest and take your stand," John wrote.[7] John also used "faith" to mean the sum of Christian teaching. Here he followed Luther and others in defining the essence of that faith by the Apostles' Creed:

I believe in God the Father Almighty Creator of Heaven and earth, and in Jesus Christ, His only Son, our Lord; Who was conceived by the Holy Spirit, born of the Virgin Mary, Suffered under Pontius Pilate, was crucified, dead, and buried; He descended into hell; the third day He rose again from the dead; He ascended into Heaven, sits at the right hand of God the Father Almighty; From thence He shall come to judge the living and the dead. I believe in the Holy Spirit, the Holy

*Christian Church, the communion of saints, the
forgiveness of sins; the resurrection of the body,
and life everlasting.*[8]

Here one must wonder why John offered the Nicene
Creed to the king as a foundation for Christian beliefs, then
offered the Apostles' Creed in the text of the *Institutes*. The
Nicene Creed specifically mentioned baptism, the Apostles'
Creed did not. The Apostles' Creed specifically mentioned
that Jesus descended into hell after crucifixion, the Nicene
Creed did not. The Apostles' Creed specifically mentioned
the communion of saints, the Nicene Creed did not. These
differences apparently were not troubling to John, so why
had he used the two creeds? Possibly he preferred the
Nicene Creed for its richer development of the same beliefs.
Possibly he thought Francis I and royalty favored it. Regard-
less, John undoubtedly used the Apostles' Creed in the main
body of the *Institutes* because the Apostles' Creed was the
creed Luther used in his catechism, after which John pat-
terned his *Institutes*.

John wrote that faith was possessing in the present
what was still hoped for—a having and a not having—"a
seeing of those things which are not seen, a clarity of
things which are obscure, a presence of things absent, a
showing of things hidden."[9] John took each belief of the
Apostles' Creed and expounded on it. Reading his explanations soon removed any reader's doubt that the *Institutes*
was merely the labor of a scholar. To expound on "I believe
in God the Father Almighty Creator of Heaven and earth,"
John gushed, "Here we profess that we have complete trust

fixed in God the Father. . . Such a Father lets us worship with grateful devotion and burning love, giving ourselves completely to His obedience and honoring Him in all things."[10] "Burning love" surpassed scholarship. John fervently loved God.

"Jesus Christ, His only Son, our Lord" triggered this from John: "Christ is Jesus to us, that is, Savior" and "He fashioned to Himself a body from our body, flesh from our flesh, bones from our bones, that He might be the same as ourselves. What was proper to us He willed to belong to Himself so that what was proper to Himself might belong to us, and that He might be both Son of God and Son of Man in common with us."[11] This was deep, devotional thinking, not mere scholarship.

In the same reverent, loving terms John confessed faith in the Holy Spirit. Not only was the Holy Spirit one with the Father and the Son, but the Holy Spirit was our God, to be adored and trusted completely. Dwelling within us, the Holy Spirit awakened us to the wealth of blessings that we possessed in Christ. The Holy Spirit was a fiery God, igniting a burning love in our hearts for God and our neighbors. The fire of the Holy Spirit consumed our sinful nature. The Holy Spirit offered us wonderful gifts on earth to serve God.

And so John explained the Creed in elegant, compassionate prose. His chapter three explained prayer, epitomized by the Lord's Prayer. The sinful man hungering for Christ and salvation had to know the power of prayer. He had to know how to pray. John urged humility, the recognition that we are weak and needy. The Bible commands us to pray. It promises us answers. Yes, we are sinful, but

"God has given us His Son, Jesus Christ, to be our advocate and mediator with Him."[12] This advocate leads us to the throne of God. There we pray in a certain way:

In asking, we lay before God the desires of our heart, seeking from His goodness, first, the things which serve His glory alone, and then the things which also minister to our profit. In giving thanks, we recognize His benefits towards us and acknowledge them with praise, accrediting to His goodness all good things everywhere.[13]

Then John added biblically based advice for praying. Although the Lord's Prayer was a perfect prayer, it was not the only format for prayer. Also, though the believers should try to raise their minds to God at all times, they should rigorously set aside definite times for prayer. Always pray when first arising in the morning, advised John. Give thanks that through God's mercy you are still alive. Always pray before and after meals. Give thanks that through God's mercy you have food to sustain yourself. Always pray at bedtime. Through God's mercy you made it through the day. But the believer should also pray for help when trouble strikes. Pray thanks when good fortune comes. Never tell God what to do. Only ask. His will is everything.

Chapter four of the *Institutes* involved the sacraments. Here the mellow, loving tone of the *Institutes* changed.

eight

Yes, the tone of John Calvin's *Institutes* definitely changed with chapter four. This chapter did not reach the level of combativeness that John's later chapters carried, but it was nevertheless heated. John first broached the subject of sacraments in this chapter. He defined a sacrament as "an outward sign by which the Lord represents and testifies His good will towards us" and as "a testimony of God's grace, declared to us by an outward symbol."[1] Without God, humans are little more than animals, creatures only of the flesh. Through God's grace, He "leads us down in these same fleshly elements—to Himself! And makes us behold in the very flesh—the things of the Spirit!"[2] Humans can not only hear God's promises but also see with their very eyes God's promises.

"The sacraments are extremely important," stressed John.

Man can not encounter God directly, but only through these oral and visible symbols. But these sacraments were rare indeed. Only two of the church of Rome's seven sacraments were valid, according to John's biblical criteria: the Lord's Supper and baptism. Here John differed from Luther, who included penance as a third sacrament. John believed the sacraments alone were points of encounter with God. He anticipated objections to this opinion. Where was Holy Scripture—the "Word"—in John's theology? Where was the Holy Spirit? He wrote:

> *In place of the one blessing of God [sacraments] which they [church of Rome] preach, we emphasize three. First, the Lord teaches us in His Word. Then He confirms it in the sacraments. And lastly He shines in our minds by the light of His Holy Spirit and opens a way into our hearts for His Word and sacraments. Else would they merely beat on our ears and meet our sight without at all affecting us inwardly. . .* [3]

Then John expounded on baptism. This sacrament, of course, was a symbol of cleansing sins, of forgiveness. In baptism God's forgiveness is permanent. Subsequent sin does not destroy the grace of baptism. A second baptism is never required. Baptism bestows the purity of Christ; this purges the stains of sin. Baptism also makes the recipient one with Christ. The recipient shares in Christ's death and resurrection. "We are baptized into the mortification of our flesh. At baptism it is begun in us. Day by day we practice it. It will be perfected when we pass from this life to the Lord," wrote John.[4]

Should infants be baptized? This was a flaming issue of the day because of the very active Anabaptists who opposed baptizing infants. Yes, John answered, infants should be baptized. Who could read Mark 10:13–16 and be foolish enough to exclude children from cleansing? That passage read:

People were bringing little children to Jesus to have him touch them, but the disciples rebuked them. When Jesus saw this, he was indignant. He said to them, "Let the little children come to me, and do not hinder them, for the kingdom of God belongs to such as these. I tell you the truth, anyone who will not receive the kingdom of God like a little child will never enter it." And he took the children in his arms, put his hands on them and blessed them. (Mark 10:13–16 NIV)

Then John discussed the Sacrament of the Last Supper, that ancient ritual in which the believer received bread, then wine. Even loyalists to the church of Rome quarreled among themselves over the nature of the Last Supper, or Eucharist. However, the intent of the Sacrament—the giving and receiving of Christ's body and blood, in effect the union with Christ—was not contentious. Through the giving and the union, Christ and His blessings are transferred to the believers. Jesus said not just "This is my body. . . this is my blood" but also "take. . . eat. . . drink," noted John, and he continued, "the whole force of the sacrament lies in what follows: 'which was given for you,' 'which was shed for you.' "[5]

What was contentious only to theologians was "how did it happen?" Theologians had argued over this concept for centuries. The official teaching of the church of Rome in the sixteenth century said the bread and wine did indeed miraculously become the body and blood of Christ. This doctrine came to be called *transubstantiation*. Another view within the church of Rome—unofficial but not heretical—held that the body and blood of Christ co-existed with the bread and wine. This view was called *consubstantiation*. The dominant figure of the Reformation, Luther, settled on a form of consubstantiation. However, the followers of Zwingli vociferously opposed Luther in their insistence that Christ was present only spiritually. So the first generation of Reformers also quarreled over the nature of the Lord's Supper.

John had to address the question. He wrote:

> *Inquisitive men have wanted to define: How the Body of Christ is present in the bread. Some, to display their subtlety, added to the simplicity of Scripture that He is present really and substantially. Others wanted to go farther, that He is present in the same dimensions as He hung on the Cross. Others invented the unnatural monster of transubstantiation. Some said the bread was the Body; some that the Body was within or under the bread; some that the bread was only a sign and figure of the Body. A matter well worth all the words and the quarrels!—or so it is commonly thought. But those who do so think do not realize that the primary question in fact is: How does the Body of Christ, as it was given for us, become ours? How does the Blood, as it was shed for us, become ours? In other words, how do we possess*

> *the whole Christ crucified and become partakers*
> *of all His blessings? Because this primary ques-*
> *tion has been omitted as unimportant, in fact*
> *neglected and almost forgotten, the conflict has*
> *raged over the one obscure and difficult question:*
> *How is the Body eaten by us?*[6]

John was in fact chastising the disputants. They had forgotten the essence of the sacrament. Did they ask minute details on how the Virgin conceived the Lord? Did they insist on knowing how the Word of God created light? Did they demand to know how Christ rose from the dead? No. For some reason they did not. The answers cannot be determined from the Bible. Then why did these disputants insist on knowing how the bread and the wine changed into the body and the blood of the Lord? This dispute only weakened the unity of the believers. Could they not be satisfied in just knowing that the Lord's Supper unified them with Christ and His blessings? Did they not recall that in Holy Scripture Christ said of the Last Supper ritual, "Do this in remembrance of me." (Luke 22:19 NIV)

Besides a remembrance, the Last Supper also served as a communion of believers, an inspiration to live in Christ. Certainly the sacrament was never given by Christ to divide the believers. John warned, "We cannot hurt, slander, mock, despise, or in any way offend one of our brethren without at the same time hurting, slandering, mocking, despising Christ in him. We cannot be at variance with our brethren without at the same time being at variance with Christ. We cannot love Christ without loving Him in our brethren."[7]

John then raised his level of combativeness to discuss
the Catholic Mass, in which the Lord's Supper was the key
ritual. His calm, reasoned writing now became much more
like the typical inflammatory writing of the times. He
wrote with heat because he now condemned the concept of
offering the Lord's Supper as the "sacrifice of the Mass."
John did nothing less than charge the church of Rome with
"destroying salvation, the atonement, and the sacraments;
it is blasphemy against Christ, the eternal High Priest."[8]
Christ sacrificed Himself once and for all. His sacrifice
does not require renewal. John's views were based on rel-
evant passages in the Epistle to the Hebrews.

First he quoted Hebrews 13:9–10:

*Do not be carried away by all kinds of strange
teachings. It is good for our hearts to be strength-
ened by grace, not by ceremonial foods, which are
of no value to those who eat them. We have an altar
from which those who minister at the tabernacle
have no right to eat.* (Hebrews 13:9–10 NIV)

Then he quoted Hebrews 13:15–16:

*Through Jesus, therefore, let us continually
offer to God a sacrifice of praise—the fruit of lips
that confess his name. And do not forget to do good
and to share with others, for with such sacrifices
God is pleased.* (Hebrews 13:15–16 NIV)

So, if there is a sacrifice in the Lord's Supper, it is a

"sacrifice of praise and thanksgiving, a sacrifice of the self-consecration of the community."[9]

What should the communicant think during the Lord's Supper? The believer should reflect on the danger of his own situation. The believer should ask "Do I completely trust Christ who now offers Himself to me?" "Do I confess my faith in Christ?" And, "Am I ready to submit to my community of believers and join them in the body of Christ?" The church of Rome expected a condition of contrition and confession to make one worthy of even participating in the Lord's Supper. John insisted that the participant only come in humility, admitting his unworthiness. Participation in the Lord's Supper was through God's mercy. John capped this discussion by suggesting the Lord's Supper be observed in every meeting of the church, just as the reading of the Bible, prayers, and almsgiving were observed in every meeting. Never should the Lord's Supper be observed in private meetings.

In the next chapter of the *Institutes,* John retained his heat in denying the status of sacraments to five rites recognized by the church of Rome as sacraments: confirmation, penance, extreme unction, holy orders, and marriage. Only God has the authority to institute a sacrament, which must be conveyed in His Word. John did not discourage evangelicals from observing these five rites, but they must not regard them as sacraments. Sacraments are the way to salvation. God, not man, dictates the means of salvation. John wrote that "the first rule of the minister is that he shall do nothing without command."[10]

John did not dwell much in his first edition of the *Institutes* on the rite of confirmation, that ritual of publicly accepting the faith. Nor did he belabor "extreme unction," that rite with oils performed on the sick or dying. In the same vein, he had little to say about marriage. Marriage of course was a good thing, but it was not a means for salvation. John was much more concerned about the two rites of penance and holy orders. These, too, were good things—but not in the way the church of Rome abused them. The rite of holy orders, or ordination of clergy, was certainly not necessary for man's salvation.

The abuse of penance by the church of Rome in their notorious sales of indulgences had ignited Luther and the Reformation. But even without indulgences, John did not like the way penance was practiced by the church of Rome. Just as in the Holy Supper, the participants in penance must not agonize on their own purity or readiness to participate. For penance, simply confess sin and repent. Believers in John's age called it "mortification of the flesh." It was humiliation, shame, and remorse for sinning. Penance was a way to be born again. In *Institutes* John wrote:

> *The way for men to be born again is to partic-*
> *ipate in Christ, in whose death their perverted*
> *desires died, on whose cross their old man was*
> *crucified, in whose sepulchre was buried the body*
> *of sin. . . The life of a Christian man is therefore a*
> *perpetual study and practice of mortifying the flesh.*[11]

The way the penitent became obsessed with the quality of his contrition disturbed John. He warned the penitent must be contrite to receive forgiveness, but not obsessed with how to achieve that aim. On the other hand, evangelicals should "teach the sinner to look, not at his compunction, nor at his tears, but to fix his gaze—both eyes!—on the sole mercy of the Lord."[12] John objected to the church of Rome's demand to enumerate and then categorize sins.

In the first place, it is simply an impossibility; and therefore it can only destroy, condemn, confound, cast into ruin and desperation. Secondly, it will divert sinners from a true realization of their sin and make them hypocrites, ignorant of God and of themselves. They will be so busy with the enumeration of their sins in detail that they will forget the hidden bottomless bog of their vices, their hidden iniquities and inward uncleanness.[13]

There was no better-known example of this needless turmoil than Luther, who as a monk tortured himself for years with imagined sins. Luther later recalled, "I know a man who has often, though only for brief periods, suffered the pains of hell such as no tongue or pen could describe and no one could believe, if he had not himself felt them. If they had lasted for a half or even a tenth part of an hour, he would have perished altogether and his bones would have crumbled to ashes."[14] But although Luther was not sinless, he had no sin to justify the magnitude of his self-torture. He was blessed with a wise mentor, Vicar von Staupitz. Von Staupitz had finally exploded, "You must have a catalogue with real sins written in it if Christ is to help you. You must not go about with such trifles and trumpery and make a sin out of every inadvertence."[15]

The true sacrament of penitence was baptism, noted John. The church of Rome invented a second sacrament of penance, so "anyone who has by sinning soiled the robe of innocence received in baptism can restore it by Penance. . . . As if Baptism were wiped out by sin and ought not rather to be recalled to the sinner's mind whenever he thinks of the forgiveness of sins, so as to take heart and courage from it and confirm his faith that the forgiveness of sins promised in Baptism will be realized. And so you will speak most aptly if you call Baptism the sacrament of repentance."[16]

John's last chapter, chapter five, discussed Christian liberty, church government, and civil government. Consider Christian liberty, stressed John, a necessary part of the Faith for two reasons. The Christian is able to have a good and clear conscience. And having that, the Christian acts boldly and confidently, not hampered by doubt. To achieve liberty, the Christian understands three things:

1. The Christian is free from Old Testament Law.
2. The Christian tries to follow the teachings Christ and His followers set forth in the New Testament. But even these commandments do not enslave the Christian.
3. Regarding the good or evil of ways of living, John had this to say:

> *If someone begins to doubt whether it is lawful*
> *for him to use linen for his sheets or shirts or hand-*
> *kerchiefs. . . he will go on to become uncertain. . .*
> *about using even canvas. For he will think to himself,*
> *". . . Do I really need to carry a handkerchief?"*
> *If it should occur to a man that some rather*

> *pleasant food was unlawful, he will get to the point*
> *of not being able to eat black bread or common*
> *dishes without an uneasy conscience before God, for*
> *it will occur to him that he could nourish his body*
> *on food yet more humble. If he is doubtful about a*
> *fairly good wine, he will then not be able to drink*
> *some rot-gut with a good conscience, and in the end*
> *he will dare touch no water that is sweeter and purer*
> *than usual. And at last such a man will think it a sin*
> *to step over a straw on the path, as they say. . . .*[17]

This sentiment of John's is the antithesis of what later came to be called Puritanism. Yet in the centuries to come, people ignorant of what John Calvin actually expressed in the *Institutes* would label him an austere Puritan.

Regarding the church and civil governments, John considered them complementary. He regarded church officials as having no power to punish. This was the realm of civil government. Within the church, he recognized in his first edition of the *Institutes* only two biblically based church officials: pastors and deacons. Pastors would take an oath and be subject to review by civil authorities. Deacons were appointed within the church body.

Certainly at this point in John's development, his concept of Christianity differed very little from Martin Luther's. Later scholars like Francois Wendel would comment that in the first edition of *Institutes*—that is, the 1536 edition—a reader familiar with Luther would have thought John Calvin was indeed "a Lutheran of southern Germany."[18] John agreed completely with Luther's central teachings on the justification of faith and regeneration by faith. He also agreed with Luther on the total perversion of sinful man, on sinning and original sin, on Christ the unique Savior and mediator, on the appropriation of salvation through the Holy Spirit, the Word, and the sacraments.

He even at this point agreed with Luther on the nature of Christ in the Last Supper and on predestination, although John had barely touched on predestination. Had John been influenced by Philip Melanchthon, Luther's right-hand man? Melanchthon in his *Loci Communes*, or "General Beliefs," had ignored predestination as an issue. Was it of small importance? Or was it an issue too contentious to include? For whichever reason, John also had little to say about predestination and remained silent as well on Luther's rejection of certain books of the Bible. John probably knew the Old Testament better than any of the earlier Reformers. Above all, though, he revered the Bible. This is the tribute he gave Holy Scriptures in *Institutes*:

> *Read Demosthenes or Cicero, read Plato,*
> *Aristotle, or any others of that class; I grant you*
> *that you will be attracted, delighted, moved, and*
> *enraptured by them in a surprising manner; but if,*
> *after reading them, you turn to the perusal of the*
> *sacred volume, whether you are willing or unwill-*
> *ing, it will affect you so powerfully, it will so pene-*
> *trate your heart, and impress itself so strongly on*
> *your mind, that, compared with its energetic influ-*
> *ence, the beauties of rhetoricians and philosophers*
> *will almost entirely disappear; so that it is easy to*

115

perceive something divine in the sacred Scriptures, which far surpasses the highest attainments and ornaments of human industry.[19]

What John had produced for evangelicals in the *Institutes* was found nowhere else in one book. Luther's work was magnificent—the inspiration of millions—but it was scattered in many publications. And even these publications, if combined, were not of one cloth. Some were written in the fury of battle and some in the serenity of peace. Melanchthon's *Loci Communes,* published in 1521, was not a comprehensive development of beliefs. It fell far short of a complete treatment of evangelicalism. Another evangelical, Zwingli, wrote in 1525 his *Commentarius de vera et falsa religions,* but "Commentaries on the true and false religions" was not even of the same quality and breath as *Loci Communes.* In 1534, William Farel had written an even smaller work, *Sommaire,* a "Summary" for Christian living, and it was printed only in French. Clearly John's comprehensive work was much needed. His *Institutes,* which was over five hundred pages in length, was to be printed in a small format so that it could be carried about. Many readers would probably think John's conclusions in the *Institutes* were completely derivative of the earlier Reformers, especially Luther and Melanchthon. But, in fact, John's head teemed with controversies he had not addressed in his *Institutes.* He could easily double or triple the size of his first *Institutes.* He was already working on a revision.

But first he delivered his *Institutes* to the printer, then took a mysterious trip to Italy.

nine

In March 1536 John Calvin, with friend Louis du Tillet, rode across the Swiss Plateau, then threaded through mountain valleys of the mighty Alps to a high, airy pass. From there they descended into the vast, green Po Valley. Near the mouth of the Po River was the ducal province of Ferrara. The duchess was twenty-six-year-old Princess Renee, the daughter of deceased French King Louis XII. In 1527, England's Cardinal Woolsey had journeyed to France to try to arrange a marriage between Princess Renee and stormy Henry VIII. Yet the royal grapevine speculated Henry VIII was really planning on somehow marrying one of the two Boleyn sisters, Anne or Mary. Henry did eventually marry Anne Boleyn. So Renee missed that death sentence.

"Henry VIII has a nasty habit of murdering wives if

they do not speedily deliver him a son," noted later cynics.

Instead, in 1528 Princess Renee married Ercole d'Este, who became duke of Ferrara in 1534. Renee could still claim the modest duchy of Chartres in France. Renee emulated Marguerite, the independent sister of Francis I. If the situation became too hot for dissidents even in the court of Marguerite, they moved on to the court of Renee. The brilliant Latin poet Clément Marot, who had persistently flouted church authority, joined Renee in 1535. Like Marguerite, Renee was still in the church of Rome but very free thinking. John Calvin's intentions in the court of the duchess remained unknown. Did he seek a place in her court? Did John still covet the life of a quiet scholar? It seems likely.

"Wherever else I had gone," he wrote later in a commentary, "I had taken care to conceal that I was the author of [the *Institutes*]; and I had resolved to continue in the same privacy and obscurity. . . my heart was set upon devoting myself to private studies, for which I wished to keep myself free from other pursuits. . . ."[1]

But John's timing was unfortunate. The court of Renee became a very unwise place to be in April 1536. One of Renee's guests openly flouted the church of Rome. Suddenly the court was besieged by angry local officials, including the duke himself. John had no desire to become a prisoner of the local nobility, perhaps to be used in a trade with French nobility. Perhaps to be delivered back to France for execution. So he departed. His only accomplishment in Ferrara was winning the friendship and confidence of Renee.

Once back in Basel he did not remain long. He next traveled to France, not now concerned about capture as long as he remained peaceful. For at the end of May, the king proclaimed the Edict of Lyons, which permitted heretics to live in France if they reconciled with the church of Rome within six months. This gave John just the window of safety he needed. With the help of Antoine, he sold the inherited family land. The proceeds were distributed, and John resigned himself to leaving Noyon for the last time. He convinced Antoine, his half sister Maria, and others in sympathy with evangelicalism to accompany him not to Basel but to Strasbourg.

"Martin Bucer and our relative Olivetan live there."

Brother Charles was not one of John's entourage. By 1536 Charles, long since excommunicated and shunned, was nearly dead. His erratic, hostile behavior suggests Charles was either going mad or was a heavy drinker. He was given to loudly abuse the church of Rome. It is probable he was not a committed dissident, but instead a man increasingly bitter against the Catholic Church that discarded him and his father. And spending his last days in a German-speaking town like Strasbourg probably had little appeal to him.

In July 1536, John's small entourage found their route to Strasbourg shut off by skirmishing troops. The emperor Charles V and Francis I were battling once again. The emperor, who had coerced the pope into supporting him, was driving fifty thousand troops up the Rhone River from the south. He hoped to cut off troops of Francis I in Savoy. The great armies were farther south, but troops were scuttling about France everywhere. John's close friends, Joachim and

Yves d'Hangest, had taken up arms for France in the conflict. In some areas, the French nobility were torching their own countryside, so the emperor's troops would have no local food supply. Naturally, if an army could not eat, neither could the local inhabitants eat.

Are not the civil and the church authorities hopeless? John must have thought of those currently in power.

Even Basel was blocked off. The detour led John's small group eventually to Geneva, where he contacted his old companion Louis du Tillet. John had resolved to spend no more than "a single night in that city."[2] Geneva had a reputation for internal religious warfare. Also, they had a complex government of "councils": the Little Council, the Two Hundred, and the General Council. Unlike Luther's remote Wittenberg, Geneva was a noted city of commerce. Geneva was ideally located to thrive on trade transactions among Switzerland, France, and Italy. As early as 1526 the city, led by Francois de Bonnivard, had set up the many councils that ruled the city in defiance of both the church of Rome and the local duke. Geneva considered itself a separate and completely independent city-state.

Geneva signed a pact with two other city-states: Catholic Fribourg and evangelical Bern. Geneva learned Fribourg was secretly plotting to undermine the new city-state. So they broke the pact with Fribourg. Egged on by the church of Rome, the local duke besieged Geneva and gained control. Evangelical Bern honored the pact and retaliated. The Bernese army recaptured the city. The angry councils declared Geneva a city of evangelicalism. This triumph of evangelicalism was news to John Calvin. It had occurred only two months before he arrived. Nevertheless, John worried that Geneva still had "ungodly and dangerous factions."[3]

The spiritual leader of Geneva was William Farel, a forty-seven-year-old protégé of the Bible scholar Jacques Lefèvre d'Étaples. The king's sister Marguerite protected Lefèvre and other mild dissidents in her court. But the younger dissidents like John and Farel were not mild. They had abandoned the church, or from their viewpoint, had been thrown out of the church. Farel had taken to preaching the gospel of the evangelicals. With a powerful speaking voice, he had enchanted crowds in Geneva for four years.

"The powerful of Geneva once called me a 'Lutheran dog,' " he shrugged.

Like Luther and Melanchthon, he and his cohorts wasted no time in exercising power. Farel assumed his power through the councils. The pope was denounced as the Antichrist. The Catholic Mass was banned by the councils. All church property was now run by Farel and his evangelicals. They removed all icons from the churches. Education was now free for everyone. But these changes were not offered as options. They were all mandatory. Yes, education was free but it was also compulsory. Yes, the church service was now evangelical, but it was also compulsory. In short, where the church of Rome once ruled, now the church of the evangelical Reformers ruled.

Little of this appealed to John. He wanted to get to Strasbourg and join Olivetan in biblical studies. But du Tillet broadcast his presence. John found himself confronted by Farel, small but bristling with passion. His eyes burned with zeal. His hair and beard were flaming red. It was clear

William Farel had decided this young scholar who had written the *Institutes* was just the man Geneva needed. Not only
did John articulate his thoughts in beautiful prose, but he
wrote boldly and with authority. Plus John had the organized, logical mind of a man trained in law. The evangelicals
had much to organize and administrate in Geneva.

Farel overwhelmed John, who would later write:

> [Farel] detained me at Geneva, not so much by
> counsel and exhortation, as by a dreadful curse,
> which I felt to be as if God had from heaven laid
> His mighty hand upon me to arrest me.... [Farel]
> burned with an extraordinary zeal to advance the
> gospel, immediately strained every nerve to detain
> me. Finding that he gained nothing by entreaties,
> he proceeded to utter the imprecation that God
> would curse my retirement and the tranquility of
> the studies which I sought, if I should withdraw and
> refuse to help, when the necessity was so urgent. By
> this imprecation I was so terror-struck, that I gave
> up the journey I had undertaken.... [4]

Not so incredibly, John remained. Geneva was an
ancient lake town, still displaying stilted houses on the
southern shores of Lake Geneva. The lake emptied to the
west into the Rhône, as did the Arves River that skirted
Geneva to the southwest. Within the city walls, Geneva was
dominated by its enormous cathedral of Saint Pierre, or St.
Peter. Every morning the more than ten thousand citizens
awakened to thunderous gongs of its giant bell called "La

Clemence." Geneva, being a town of merchants and traders, had few nobility. Perhaps they did not care to live in such a place, because wealthy Geneva was often attacked. Certainly few dared lived outside the walls. So land within was precious. Only the very wealthy who lived along the rue des Chanoines, Place Saint Pierre, les Allemandes, and la Riviere had gardens of any size.

That summer, John continued to revise and expand his *Institutes*. The fact that his first edition in Latin had sold so well proved it was much needed. And his mind teemed with improvements. But he had also agreed to be a reader in theology. So as a "Reader of Holy Scripture" and not a pastor, John gave his first sermon in the church of Saint Pierre on September 5, 1536. John spoke on the epistles of Paul. This focus on Paul was characteristic of evangelicals. After all, it was Paul's Book of Romans—with its promise that righteousness from God "is by faith from first to last" (Romans 1:17 NIV)—that had nurtured the seed of rebellion in Martin Luther. In many ways, the evangelicals embraced the teachings of Paul much more than the church of Rome did.

"Lausanne is on the brink," announced the fiery Farel one day.

So in October 1536, John went with Farel and Pierre Viret, another prominent evangelical, to Lausanne. This Swiss city, on the north shore of Lake Geneva, still was in a state of flux over the Reformation. John played a minor part in a disputation there. However, the evangelicals from Geneva convinced Lausanne to become an evangelical city. Back in Geneva, the evangelicals wrestled with the question of the church's role in enforcing morality. The Catholic Church in conjunction with the civil authorities had always possessed that authority. Yet they had looked the other way at sin. Many citizens of Geneva indulged in dancing, drinking, gambling, and adultery. One district of the city was occupied by brothels, where women sold their bodies. The ruler of this district was called the "Brothel Queen." Were the evangelicals going to ignore all this sinful behavior like the Catholics had?

"Do you dare move against it?" asked their detractors.

John and his colleagues were not in doubt. The Bible very definitely condemned those kinds of sin. Such behavior was to be no more tolerated than such behavior was tolerated in ancient Israel. To ignore these sins was in itself sinful. They who possessed authority were obligated to enforce the moral code of the Bible. This did not mean they were powerful. Power did not even really reside in their office. Nor did power reside in inspiration from the Word of God. The power was in the *actual* Word of God. And only Christ knew the secrets of the Father. John wrote:

> *By it [the Word of God] they confidently dare all things, compel all the strength, glory, and sublimity of the world to submit to its majesty and to obey it, rule over all things from the highest to the lowest, build up the house of Christ, overturn the kingdom of Satan, feed the sheep, destroy the wolves, exhort and instruct the teachable, rebuke, reprove, and refute the rebellious and stubborn,*

*loose, bind, and finally, hurl thunderbolts—but
doing all things in the Word of God. . .[5]*

"So let Christ speak and all be silent!" they concluded.

The evangelicals, of course, rejected the Roman code of law, so they had to translate the Word of God in the Bible— found in the teachings of Christ—into a civil code. Christ's Word was without error. The first things the evangelicals did were to issue, in November 1536, Farel's "Confession of Faith and Discipline" and John's "Catechism." The councils approved them, and required all citizens to swear to uphold these beliefs. This was the cost of remaining in Geneva.

"Discipline is essential to the life of the church," insisted the evangelicals.

But John urged caution. Also, he asked representatives of the new evangelical church not to be influenced in their enforcement of Christ's teachings by external factors. Never rely on superstitions, or customs not of God's Word. Always build up the local church. On the other hand, do not criticize other churches with different customs. The church must use God's Word for the salvation of men and women. The church must serve, not tyrannize.

Authority within the confines of the church itself should have been uncontroversial. John did not think anyone would question Paul's injunctions that women cover their heads and not preach the Gospels. Why would anyone resent kneeling for prayer or shrouding the dead for burial? The representatives of the church also had a right to determine the days and times of its services, as well as to determine which hymns and chants to use. Singing and chanting gave fire to prayers that otherwise tended to be cold and lifeless. Because this was new, a children's choir sang clearly as a guide. Of course every service had both a sermon and collection of funds. In John's *Institutes,* he advised every church service to also include the Lord's Supper. His colleagues felt this was too often. They agreed on once a month. But because the various churches in Geneva held the Lord's Supper in turn, a worshipper who desired it could have the Lord's Supper every week.

They decided the purity of the Lord's Supper must not be polluted by the unrepentant. This required policing. They appointed overseers in the various districts of the city to report serious sins of the flock to the ministers of the church. The representatives of the church had the right to admonish, even to excommunicate. John cautioned that representatives must always be guided by the principle of mutual love. The actual procedure was clearly stated by Christ Himself in the Book of Matthew:

> *If your brother sins against you, go and show him his fault, just between the two of you. If he listens to you, you have won your brother over. But if he will not listen, take one or two others along, so that "every matter may be established by the testimony of two or three witnesses." If he refuses to listen to them, tell it to the church; and if he refuses to listen even to the church, treat him as you would a pagan or a tax collector. . . .*
> (Matthew 18:15–17 NIV)

This clearly mandated excommunication. The evangelicals were not going to be lax in discipline like the church of Rome was.

In 1537, John Calvin became more than a Reader of Holy Scripture. He was elected pastor. He was busy every moment. With his colleagues, he was building the foundation of their faith. He continued to revise his *Institutes*. But now he also regularly preached sermons, baptized babies, officiated at weddings, and conducted funeral rites. John was full-time pastor, not just a remote lawyer-trained planner organizing the church according to strict biblical principles. The pastoral duties only made him a better churchman.

The councils of Geneva were at first very enthused with the transition from the church of Rome to evangelicals. Not only did all citizens of Geneva have to swear to the new "Confession of Faith and Discipline," but all children had to be instructed in the Catechism and periodically tested. They also eagerly passed a civil ordinance that on Sundays during sermon time "neither butchers, nor tripe sellers, nor others, nor second hand dealers shall stay open beyond the last stroke of the great bell; that those who have idols at home break them up forthwith; that there is to be no singing of idle songs and no playing of games of chance; nor are the pastry cooks to cry their wares during the time of sermon."[6]

However, John and his colleagues discovered the councils were not so enthused in enforcing their ordinances. Many powerful citizens did not mind seeing the church of Rome run off, but on the other hand they did not want to swear an allegiance to evangelicalism, either. Yet, the oath of allegiance had become an ordinance. John and his colleagues demanded a reckoning. Unsaid was the desire of many citizens to see an end to the policing of their sins. A meeting of John and his colleagues with the councils on November 26, 1537, was contentious.

"Do you expect us to perjure ourselves?" complained one who did not want to take the oath.

"We ask only that you swear to keep to the faith of God and to follow His commandments," was the unwanted answer.

John and his friends left the meeting with no solid commitment by the councils to enforce allegiance to the Confession of Faith and Discipline. Their enemies began to plot against them. "Aren't these men all Frenchmen?" whispered their enemies. Wasn't France eager to incorporate a city of commerce like Geneva? Surely these Frenchmen must be spies! These very spies were trying to gain control of every aspect of life in Geneva. Then it would be a simple matter of inviting their French masters to rule Geneva. John and his colleagues shrugged off these attempts to smear them. Yet a group, who now called themselves "Patriots," continued to plot against them and spread lies.

Then John received more and more crosses to bear. It was bad enough that Louis du Tillet returned to France to the Catholic faith. But John learned brother Charles had died in October 1537. Poor combative Charles was officially a heretic, buried beneath the town gallows! Then John also learned his dear friends, Joachim and Yves d'Hangest, had been killed in battle. The young men were killed at the storming of Saint-Pol, a castle not fifty miles from Noyon.

Then the good intentions of the evangelicals at Geneva led to more trouble. Caroli, one of the so-called evangelical ministers in Lausanne, was observed saying prayers for the dead. Pierre Viret reported him to his local evangelical authorities. In retaliation, Caroli accused John Calvin and William Farel of promoting Arianism, a heresy that the Christ is a created being. They had to refute this lie in a disputation. Caroli was soundly defeated, resulting in his exile. He returned to France and the church of Rome. But yet another rumor had been born about John and his colleagues in Geneva.

"These evangelicals believe Christ was created," said many, eager only to be rid of these moral enforcers.

To maker matters worse, the evangelicals of Bern began to interfere in the affairs of the evangelicals of Geneva. Had they been angered by Geneva interfering at Lausanne? In any event, they had their own ways of doing church business, and they saw no reason why Geneva could not conform to their ways. Their requests seemed trivial. Baptism should be administered only at the font. The bread at the Lord's Supper should always be unleavened. Christmas, Easter, Ascension, and Pentecost should be the only great festivals observed. These were not great issues, yet John and his friends resisted. John saw these demands as a return to the old religious legalism. Besides, he and his colleagues knew more was at stake.

"This is only the first attempt of the new chief minister of the Bern church, Peter Kuntz, to extend his power," they murmured.

Unfortunately, many on the councils of Geneva were

sympathetic to the demands from Bern. Did they do this only to get rid of John and his enforcers? Then they could easily rid themselves of the Bern intruders. For by early 1538 libertines who loved their sin, Catholics who wanted to restore their faith, and the so-called Patriots came to dominate the councils. There was now much sentiment in Geneva against the evangelicals. Being required to live a sinless life was too painful for many citizens. To make matters worse for John and his friends, in February 1538 an alleged French agent was accused of trying to make a deal with two evangelicals in Geneva. Mobs gathered in the streets at night. They protested in front of the houses of the leading evangelicals. They fired guns in the air.

"Leave Geneva, Frenchmen, or die!" they screamed in the night.

Yet John and his colleagues refused to implement the demands of Bern. No, they would not cooperate. They would bring these matters up in the coming Synod at Zurich. Let that assembled body of evangelicals make a judgment. But the councils would not wait. Now apparently in complete sympathy with the intruders from Bern, they brought the situation to a head during Easter. Because the local evangelicals refused to implement the suggestions of Bern, the councils insisted John, Farel, and the other Genevan evangelicals must leave within three days!

John was stunned.

ten

John and his colleagues complied with the order to leave Geneva. Amazingly, John journeyed with William Farel to Bern. Apparently they felt non-evangelical members of the councils had only used the suggestions from Bern to get rid of them. Peter Kuntz and the rest of the Bern cadre were sympathetic, realizing that their own ambitions and interference had helped non-evangelicals undermine evangelicalism in Geneva. Nevertheless, at the subsequent Synod at Zurich, John presented fourteen articles on policies of the church, careful now to incorporate the demands of Bern. In return, Bern defended the previous procedures of John and Farel at Geneva as scriptural. The synod asked Bern to use its influence to get John and Farel restored as ministers in Geneva. But they also reprimanded the Geneva evangelicals for being too zealous in implementing changes.

"You are guilty of 'misplaced vigor,' misplaced because you were dealing with 'so undisciplined a people,' " declared the synod.[1]

With that the synod ended. John and Farel could not have hoped for more help than that. But they surely hoped for better results than the Bern mediators achieved when they finally carried out their mission in May 1538. For the councils at Geneva steadfastly refused to take the evangelicals back. So in June, John and Farel went to Basel. John's head was swimming with doubt now. Had he been mistaken in believing Geneva was God's calling for him? Surely not, he reassured himself. But later ruminations indicated he was not sure.

"After that calamity," he wrote later, "when my ministry seemed to me to be disastrous and unsuccessful, I made up my mind never again to enter on any ecclesiastical charge whatever unless the Lord should call me to it by a clear and manifest call."[2]

At Martin Bucer's invitation, John went to Strasbourg on the Rhine. This was a border city between France and Germany. In the fifteen hundreds, it was predominantly German-speaking. John had enjoyed the hospitality of Bucer there in late 1534. In 1538 he joined Bucer, now forty-six. John himself was just turning twenty-nine. Bucer was known as a peacemaker. After all, his realm lay between that of two great disputants: Zwingli to the south and Luther to the north. Zwingli was now dead, but Luther at fifty-five was still stormy and difficult. The two great camps of Reformers—those later called "Lutherans" or "evangelicals" to the north and the "Swiss Reformed" to the south—still wrestled over their differences. However, future historians would label both Bucer and John Calvin as Swiss Reformed.

John saw recent letters from Martin Luther to Bucer and his colleague Capito. The mercurial Luther's remarks were remarkably calm and conciliatory. Luther wrote on December 1, 1537, that the quarreling factions could reconcile "provided we can lay aside all that is offensive, and in like-minded agreement give room for the leading and guidance of the Holy Spirit, that we may go forward in pious and brotherly concord. Assuredly, in so far as we are concerned, and especially as regards myself, casting aside whatever may be occasion of offence, I shall embrace you in faith, good will, and with love."[3] Just five days later, another letter arrived in which Luther added, "I write these things that you may know that our heart is upright and sincere in the hope of agreement; may the Lord Himself complete the work. Amen."[4]

"So is not Brother Bucer justified in his efforts to reconcile?" reasoned his associates.

Bucer was indeed always there at every disputation as the conciliator and pragmatist. He was much like Luther's Philip Melanchthon in that respect. However he, unlike Melanchthon, considered unity the utmost priority. To reconcile differences, for example, between the Lutherans' claim that Christ was actually present in the bread and wine in the sacrament of the Last Supper and the Swiss Reformed claim that Christ was there only spiritually, Bucer had taken to using intentionally ambiguous or obscure language. He justified this by insisting doctrinal differences could be worked out later. First the evangelicals must unite. One of the great criticisms of the evangelical movement was that the reformers themselves were splintering into ever smaller contentious groups. The criticism was valid. But John well knew that very often the differences were encouraged by powerful parties that wanted the evangelical movement to disintegrate.

"Secular groups desire that," he reflected, "as does the church of Rome."

Bucer had been a Dominican monk. In 1518, he attended a public disputation in which Luther spoke. Luther was then only thirty-five, an Augustinian monk right in the midst of his emergence as a dissident. Bucer was twenty-seven and, like most who heard the fiery, articulate Luther, he was overwhelmed. Luther had everything: scholarship, commitment, piety, eloquence, and courage. But most of all to Bucer everything Luther said made sense. Three years later, Bucer left the Dominicans and adopted evangelicalism. Over the years, he had risen in prominence among the German evangelicals but could not rival Luther or Melanchthon. One reason was that although Bucer wrote volumes of material, he published very little.

Bucer encouraged John to stay in Strasbourg. John asked Bucer to invite Farel, too. Bucer refused. So John refused Bucer's invitation to stay. Apparently Bucer knew that among evangelical leaders, the wisdom now was that John and Farel were gifted but ministering together they were poison. "One urges on the other," wrote John to Farel later of the criticism of their collaboration.[5] But Bucer persisted in recruiting John. Perhaps Bucer had learned how Farel had bullied the mild-tempered, often indecisive John

Calvin to reside in Geneva. And indeed John returned to Strasbourg for a second visit. On this the second visit, Bucer thundered that John was refusing God's call. "Are you not ashamed that so great an assemblage remains silent?" accused Bucer, referring to hundreds of Strasbourg evangelicals who needed a pastor.[6] Surely because of that refusal, suggested Bucer, John's much desired scholarship would never prosper. That startled John. Yes, perhaps he would be refusing God's call.

In his most secret moments perhaps he postulated, "Is anyone else but Martin Bucer pleading for my services?"

In the meantime, Farel accepted a pastorate in Neuchâatel, about eighty miles northeast of Geneva. Like Geneva it was also on the Swiss border with France. John felt free now. Farel was placed. John had no reason whatever now to refuse Strasbourg. So in September 1538, he took a meager-salaried pastorate of about five hundred French-speaking evangelicals in Strasbourg. "I can't call a single penny my own," he recorded not in self-pity but in genuine astonishment.[7] Every penny seemed to disappear into the pastorate. He sustained himself by selling many of his books and also taking boarders into his rectory. Only occasionally did he practice law. "I have my own share of contests and wrestlings where I am, and most arduous they are," he wrote. "But they do not overwhelm me; they merely keep me in training."[8] Yes, he was content. He was a French pastor for a French-speaking congregation. He preached every day, with two sermons on Sunday.

He was a strict pastor. Once a month he offered the Lord's Supper. But the prior week, all who intended to participate had to see him. He saw them for three reasons. First, it allowed him to explain the profound significance of the sacrament. Second, he warned them to approach the altar in the purity of repentance. Lastly, he ministered to those who were troubled, perhaps doubting if they were in the right state for participation. And, indeed, he determined some were not pure enough for participation. As pastor he was obligated to exclude unrepentant sinners. One of his candidates for the sacrament sneered that John was trying to reintroduce the confession rite of the church of Rome. John remained firm.

"You are known to be a gambler and an adulterer," he told the complainer, "but worse, you are unrepentant."

On the other hand, John did not conduct a gloomy, somber church of Rome service. He introduced congregational singing. By 1539, his worshippers sang from a metrical psalter in French. One French-speaking man, who had fled to Strasbourg from the Netherlands, wrote of John's church:

> *Everyone sings, men and women, and it is a lovely sight. Each has a music book in his hand. . . For five or six days at the beginning as I looked on this little company of exiles, I wept, not for sadness but for joy to hear them all singing so heartily, and as they sang giving thanks to God that He had led them to a place where His name is glorified. No one could imagine what joy there is in singing the praises and wonders of the Lord in the mother tongue as they are sung here.[9]*

So, although John was strict, he was also a gifted and sensitive pastor. He also lectured in public on theology. At the time, he was particularly enthused about three of his favorite books in the New Testament: the Gospel of John and Paul's books of Romans and 1 Corinthians. Still, he could not escape disputes from the outside. He sparred by letter with his old friend Louis du Tillet. Caroli, who had accused John of Arianism, reappeared to torment him. Martin Bucer humored Caroli by summoning John to a dispute with Caroli over the incident. John was stunned. He and Farel had been widely criticized for being too fervent. Now he was called into a frivolous public dispute where he might lose his temper. So he refused. But Bucer and the other evangelicals insisted he at least meet with them privately. John wrote an account of the episode to Farel:

> *I sinned grievously through not keeping my temper. For my mind was so filled with bile that I poured out bitterness on all sides. . . I could not have been ruder to Caroli himself had he been present. At last I forced myself out of the dining room. . . When I got home, I was seized with an extraordinary paroxysm and could find no relief but in tears and sighs. . . .*[10]

What an irony that future generations would think him a cold, calculating man. John was deeply upset over his inability to control his temper. But he always had his studies to calm him. The *Institutes* was a lifetime commitment. He would never stop improving it. How could he? Christianity was infinitely rich. In 1539, he found out that tragically he had inherited the superb library of his relative Pierre Robert. Olivetan had died, only thirty-three, on a trip to visit Duchess Renee of Ferrara in Italy. Fortunately John's financial situation had improved. He would not have to sell any of Olivetan's precious books. It was at this time, and perhaps earlier, as well, that John tried to incorporate every predecessor who had insight to bear on the doctrines of the *Institutes.* He used the great Greek philosopher Plato. He noted many fathers of the early church, including Origen. He acknowledged Peter Lombard and his *Sentences,* the great Catholic work of the Middle Ages. But more than anyone, he incorporated the ideas and interpretations of Augustine. He had quoted Augustine fifteen times in *De Clementia,* his 1532 commentary on Seneca, so he had already demonstrated a deep respect for this genius of the early church.

Augustine was born in North Africa in A.D. 354. His mother was Christian, but Augustine remained pagan for many years. A brilliant scholar, he acquired a classical education in both Carthage and Rome. At the age of thirty-two, he had a mystical experience and accepted Christ. Later he wrote of his experiences in *Confessions,* a book surpassed only by the Bible in brilliance and passion. More than anyone else, Augustine tried to fuse the philosophy of Plato with Christianity. His writings—all in Latin—were dazzling in eloquence and logic. *City of God* and many other writings established him as the theological giant of the postbiblical church. In addition, Augustine virtually invented the analysis—or exegesis—of Scriptures. His interpretations were profound, apparently irrefutable. It seemed every churchman who ever read the works of Augustine was in awe. Catholics were no exceptions. Martin Luther was no exception. Nor was John Calvin.

Excerpts from Augustine's various early writings prove that prior to the age of about sixty-five, he was very definite in his belief in free will. In a very early treatise, *Of True Religion,* he wrote, "In fact, sin is so much a voluntary evil that it is not sin at all unless it is voluntary."[10] In *Two Souls, Against the Manichaeans,* another treatise written about the same time, he also repeatedly confirmed free will. He stated, "For every one also who does a thing unwillingly is compelled, and every one who is compelled, if he does a thing, does it only unwillingly. It follows that he that is willing is free from compulsion, even if any one thinks himself compelled."[11] In the same work he also wrote, "Sin is indeed nowhere but in the will, since this consideration also would have helped me, that justice holds guilty those sinning by evil will alone, although they may have been unable to accomplish what they willed."[12] And yet again in *Two Souls, Against the Manichaeans,* he declared the innocence of anyone compelled to do something: ". . . whoever has done anything evil by means of one unconscious or unable to resist, the latter can by no means be justly condemned."[13]

Twenty years later Augustine still supported free will. In *On the Spirit and the Letter,* he wrote that "Free will, naturally assigned by the creator to our rational soul, is such a neutral power, as can either incline toward faith, or turn toward unbelief."[14] Moreover, in his masterpiece *City of God,* he addressed very directly the conundrum of predestination related to God's foreknowledge: "We are by no means under compulsion to abandon free choice in favor of divine knowledge, nor need we deny—God forbid!—that God knows the future, as a condition for holding free choice."[15] Augustine further stated in *City of God,* "For, no one sins because God foreknew that he would sin. In fact, the very reason why a man is undoubtedly responsible for his own sin, when he sins, is because He whose foreknowledge cannot be deceived foresaw, not the man's fate or fortune or what not, but that the man himself would be responsible for his own sin. No man sins unless it is his choice to sin; and his choice not to sin, that, too, God foresaw."[16]

Prior to the age of sixty-five, Augustine left no doubt that mankind possessed free will. And this was not idle philosophical speculation. Augustine always supported his arguments with the ultimate written source: the Bible. But then came Pelagius. Fluent in both Latin and Greek, the highly educated Pelagius was not a cleric although he lived as a monk. When he began to publish, it was obvious to Augustine that he was not a Bible-believer at all. Pelagius denied the meaning of Adam and Eve, and thus the origin of sin. Lust and death were natural, not the result of sin. If sin existed, it was merely the result of Adam's poor example. Augustine saw that Pelagius was little more than a pagan, incorporating Stoicism. He was more or less an early secular humanist. Man's will power, harnessed to discipline, insisted Pelagius, was quite enough to attain the highest virtue. Christ's redemption was merely an example of "good"—a counterbalance to offset the bad example of Adam. Man had the ability to conquer sin and gain eternal life without the help of God's grace.

Pelagius was clever, though. He also used the Bible. From the Bible, he quoted passages out of context that seemed to support his contentions. From the Book of Matthew, he used Christ's words "Be perfect, therefore, as your heavenly Father is perfect" (Matthew 5:48 NIV) as proof God wanted us to be perfect. And if God wanted us to be perfect then it was possible to be perfect. The underpinning of the arguments of Pelagius was "free will." Pelagius emphasized that if an individual used his free will with discipline, he could attain perfection—without God's grace—and even attain salvation.

Of course this was heresy. Augustine reacted strongly. It is probable he also was reacting to a splinter group called the Donatists. In any event, a revolution in Augustine's thought began that may have been lost on many later scholars. Abruptly, he began to argue against free will. "Enchiridion," a handbook on Faith, Hope, and Love, burst forth with the change in A.D. 421. Augustine was sixty-seven. Free will was lost in the Garden of Eden. "For it was by the evil use of his free will that man destroyed both it and himself. For, as a man who kills himself must, of course, be alive when he kills himself, but after he has killed himself ceases to live, and cannot restore himself to life; so, when man by his own free will sinned, then sin being victorious over him, the freedom of his will was lost."[16]

In the same work, Augustine emphasized that what mankind thought was free will was actually God's will as shown by Paul's letter to the Philippians: "And further, should any one be inclined to boast, not indeed of his

141

works, but of the freedom of his will, as if the first merit belonged to him, this very liberty of good action being given to him as a reward he had earned, let him listen to this same preacher of grace, when he says: 'For it is God who works in you to will and to act according to his good purpose' [Philippians 2:13 NIV]."[17]

Certainly much of what mankind might have mistaken for their own merit, Augustine explained in "Enchiridion," was actually by God's grace. Here he enlists Paul's letter to the Ephesians: "And lest men should arrogate to themselves the merit of their own faith at least, not understanding that this too is the gift of God, this same apostle, who says in another place. . . 'For it is by grace you have been saved, through faith—and this not from yourselves, it is the gift of God—not by works, so that no one can boast' [Ephesians 2:8–9 NIV]."[18]

In "Enchiridion," Augustine even touched on the knotty subject of double-predestination, that very unpopular concept of God predetermining both the saved and the doomed: "As the Supreme Good, He made good use of evil deeds, for the damnation of those whom He had justly predestined to punishment and for the salvation of those whom He had mercifully predestined to grace." In the same work, Augustine wrote that God could turn evil wills toward the good. "Furthermore, who would be so impiously foolish as to say that God cannot turn the evil wills of men—as He wills, when He wills, and where He wills— toward the good? But when He acts, He acts through mercy; when He does not act, it is through justice."[19]

As a consequence, Augustine had to refute Bible passages

that seemed to indicate all mankind could be saved. Paul wrote in his first letter to Timothy, "This is good, and pleases God our Savior, who wants all men to be saved and to come to a knowledge of the truth," (1 Timothy 2:3–4 NIV). Augustine retorted in "Enchiridion" that "when we hear and read in Scripture that He will have all men to be saved, although we know well that all men are not saved, we are not on that account to restrict the omnipotence of God, but are rather to understand the Scripture, 'who wants all men to be saved,' as meaning that no man is saved unless God wills his salvation: not that there is no man whose salvation He does not will, but that no man is saved apart from His will; and that, therefore, we should pray to Him to will our salvation, because if He wills it, it must necessarily be accomplished."[20]

Augustine refuted a passage in Matthew with a passage from Psalm 135, "Our Lord says plainly, however, in the Gospel, when upbraiding the impious city: 'How often I have longed to gather your children together, as a hen gathers her chicks under her wings, but you were not willing' [Matthew 23:37 NIV] as if the will of God had been overcome by the will of men. . . [But] He gathered together as many of her children as He wished: for He does not will some things and do them, and will others and do them not; but 'The Lord does whatever pleases him, in the heavens and on the earth' [Psalm 135:6 NIV]."[21]

"Enchiridion" was not unique in its denial of free will. If the work had stood alone, later scholars might have concluded it was a fake or Augustine was ill at the time because it differed so radically from Augustine's earlier works. But Augustine's other later works, like *On Grace and Free Will, On Rebuke and Grace,* and later additions to *City of God,* show the same theology. God is so sovereign, He is not only the first cause of everything, He is the *only* cause of everything. Loss of free will was intertwined with all the other theological concepts. Augustine truly believed that God willed not all to be saved but willed just some. Those saved were the elect. And they were chosen before time began. They had no choice in the matter. Nor did those condemned to hell have any choice in the matter. So, some of mankind were granted faith and salvation. Some of mankind were denied faith and condemned. This naturally led to the irksome conclusion that God was not all-loving but loved only some. An all-powerful, all-loving God would save everyone or at least give everyone the free will to choose.

It was a staggering conclusion by the older Augustine.

The change in theology was not lost on John Calvin. Here was a colossal dilemma. From Irenaeus in the second century to Thomas Aquinas in the thirteenth century, the fathers of the church had embraced free will. These scholars also included no less than Justin Martyr, Tertullian, Origen, Gregory, Jerome, and Chrysostom. Only the older Augustine argued the opposite. Yet John Calvin was more convinced by the later Augustine than the early Augustine and all the church fathers. The mature Augustine was more persuasive, again always using biblical support. To John the logic of Augustine was irrefutable.

Of Augustine's early view on free will John wrote in his *Institutes,* "Even Augustine was not always free from this superstition, as when he says that blinding and hardening have respect not to the operation of God but to foreknowledge. But this subtlety is repudiated by many passages of Scripture, which clearly show that the divine interference amounts to something more than foreknowledge."[23]

Thus influenced strongly by the older Augustine, John revised the *Institutes*.

eleven

Finished in July 1539, the new *Institutes* was a major revision resulting in a work three times longer than the first edition. The second edition was "aimed at embracing a summary of religion in all its parts,"[1] and organized "to prepare and train students in theology for the study of the divine Word that they might have an easy access into it and keep on in it without stumbling."[2] Nevertheless, the *Institutes* still remained roughly organized along the lines of Luther's Catechism.

The first sentence of the main text read, "Well-nigh the sum of sacred doctrine consists in these two parts: the knowledge of God and the knowledge of ourselves."[3] It was clear now that this well-known assertion of John Calvin was also drawn from Augustine, who had emphasized that he desired to know two things only: God and the soul. The two desired subjects became the first two chapters of the *Institutes*. In the "Knowledge of God" chapter, John's articulation of the nature of the Trinity answered Caroli and other critics.

"Praise God that I have this forum to respond calmly and logically," reflected John.

Enlarged chapters on law and faith followed. Then, penitence was a chapter in its own right. More new chapters followed that: "On Justification by Faith and on the Merits of Works," "On the Likeness and Difference between the Old and New Testaments," and "On God's Predestination and Providence." Here John, heavily influenced by Augustine, developed and declared what had been unspoken presuppositions to his first edition. Chapter nine, on prayer, was an amplification of the old chapter three. Old chapter four, "On the Sacraments," became chapters ten, eleven, and twelve: "On the Sacraments," "On Baptism," and "On the Lord's Supper." The sacraments were always controversial, baptism now as much as the Last Supper. The old chapter six changed but little to chapters thirteen, fourteen, and fifteen: "On Christian Liberty," "On the Power of the Church," and "On Political Administration." The final chapter was completely new: "On the Life of the Christian Man."

"Of seventeen chapters six are new, five are expanded sections of old chapters, and six are old revised chapters," John concluded.

The two sacraments were of utmost importance. Ironically, these two biblically mandated rites had split the evangelicals into camps. Everyone wanted to unite, but no one was willing to compromise. On the sacrament of baptism, John had added in his second edition of the *Institutes* a formal defense of infant baptism. This, of course, was aimed at the practice of the Anabaptists who approved baptism only when a child reached the "age of reason."

The nature of the Lord's Supper was also a flash point with theologians. Luther's evangelicals and Zwingli's Swiss Reformed had quarreled over whether the presence of Christ was carnal or spiritual. Luther took the traditional Catholic view of carnal presence; Zwingli took the view of spiritual presence. In the first edition of *Institutes,* John seemed to side with Luther and tradition, though he stated his exasperation at the magnitude of the controversy. Now, in the second edition, he moved to an intermediate position. John affirmed communion with both the carnal presence of Christ as well as His spiritual presence, while rejecting the local presence of the body of Christ in the bread and wine. Was he influenced by the conciliator Bucer? For this was also the view of Bucer, who touted this intermediate position as reconciling the views of Luther's evangelicals and Zwingli's Swiss Reformers.

"But will Luther even read the *Institutes*?" wondered John.

The *Institutes* of 1536 caused some to conclude John was merely a follower of Luther, polishing his theological doctrines. They could no longer conclude that from the *Institutes* of 1539. John clearly differed from Luther on several points. He still agreed with Luther on the doctrines of total depravity, original sin, justification by faith alone, and the uniqueness of Christ as Savior. He also agreed on the roles of the Holy Spirit, baptism, and the Bible in aiding salvation. But now he differed with Luther on the Lord's Supper. And John took a much harder line on predestination. Luther believed God knew the elect because He was outside of time and foresaw the future. John believed God foresaw the future because He had willed it. John wrote that "no one can deny that God foreknew the future final fate of man before He created him, and that He foreknew it because it was appointed by His own decree."[4] God decreed the saved, just as He decreed the damned. John admitted that this was "a horrible decree."[5] But he could not conclude otherwise. No wonder Melanchthon avoided the issue of predestination in his writings.

Once a student mastered the *Institutes,* John reasoned in the same work, the student would move on to the Bible:

> *I think I have so embraced the sum of religion in all its parts and arranged it systematically that if anyone grasps it aright he will have no difficulty in deciding what he ought principally to seek in Scripture and to what end he should refer everything in it. Thus I have, as it were, paved the way. And if I shall hereafter publish any commentaries on Scripture, I shall always condense them and keep them short, for I shall not need to undertake lengthy discussions on doctrines or digress into loci communes. By this method the godly reader will be spared great trouble and boredom, provided he approaches [the commentaries] forearmed with a knowledge of the present work as a necessary weapon. . . .[6]*

Because his revised *Institutes* so strongly pointed the student toward interpreting the Bible, it was no surprise John was already writing and planning commentaries. He had found Melanchthon's commentaries far too skimpy. John wanted not only to investigate the Scriptures linguistically, grammatically, and historically, but to also assure a theological understanding. Yet he aimed at brevity, too, declaring, "the chief virtue of an interpreter lies in clear brevity."[7]

"I know only too well the Bible student's hopeless task of using one of Bucer's massive commentaries," he admitted to himself.

With lofty goals for his commentaries, John had set out to do Paul's Book of Romans so that it would be available not long after the revised *Institutes* appeared. And indeed his commentary on Romans appeared in March 1540. All subsequent commentaries were to follow the same format. The commentary began with the Argumentum, or theme, of the biblical book. This included a brief statement of the doctrine, as well as any questions regarding date and authorship. Then followed the text of the book or epistle. In John Calvin's day, the text was divided only into chapters; there was as yet no system that subdivided chapters into verses. John broke the chapters into paragraphs, the definitive text being in Greek. John used various Greek texts, including those of Erasmus (1527), Colines (1534), and one dubbed "Polyglot" (1522). The Latin translation of the Greek text was his own. For John still published works essentially in Latin.

"Though I will someday finish my French version of the '*Institutes*,' " he promised.

The text and translation of the commentary established, John wrote his exegesis and exposition. Many questions had to be explored. What did the passage mean within the framework of the chapter or even the entire book? What was the historical setting? Was it a time of peace? Or tribulation? What particular literary form of the Bible was it: straight historical narrative or prophetic literature or allegory or instruction or some other genre? Also, the text had to be investigated on at least three levels: the original meaning, the meaning to Jesus and His followers, and the meaning to the contemporary Christian.

"And I will use and credit any past wisdom I find useful," he mused.

He used contemporaries like Melanchthon, Luther, and Erasmus. He used Scholastic scholars of the Middle Ages. He used the old church fathers like Chrysostom and Augustine. He used the Jewish historian Josephus, the Latin historian Pliny. He mined dozens of sources. If he neglected any aspect of exegesis, it was the development of the ancient settings. In this he was like Luther. He focused on what it meant to his contemporary Christians. How did they apply the teachings of the Bible? John believed the Bible was a gift of God. The Bible was God's revelation. God would not have made it obscure. So John tended to be literal in his interpretations. Here he differed from his beloved Augustine, who loved to apply complex allegories.

"But if God gave the Word to mankind," critics asked, "why did the Bible exhibit peculiarities of literary style, seeming contradictions, and even inaccuracies?"

"Men are imperfect, trying to convey the most profound

thoughts of the Creator in mere human languages," answered John.

In 1540 John was still only thirty-one years old. His friends began to champion the cause of marriage. John, although he worked every waking minute, thought marriage might be an excellent idea. Ever the meticulous scholar, he made a list of attributes he desired in a wife. She need not be beautiful or even comely.

"I am not one of those insane lovers who, when once smitten with the fine figure of a woman, embrace also her faults," he warned his cupids.[8]

But it *was* essential she possess purity, patience, and the good sense to run a household, John added matter-of-factly. Luther had found exactly that kind of wife. Catherine van Bora ran his house like a clock, nursed him, bore his children, even gardened and farmed! John thought that must be a superb arrangement for a busy man. The more he thought about it the more anxious he became.

"Set out at once," he wrote excitedly when informed there was just such a woman for him.[9]

But that attempt fell short. Others also failed for various reasons. But by August 1540 a marriage had been arranged. The woman was an attractive widow, Idelette de Bure, with a son and daughter. Her husband had been an Anabaptist whom John had converted to his form of evangelicalism. Idelette did not disappoint him. John probably had not been happier since his student days at Orléans. He pastored, studied, and wrote. His writing had never been better. His Latin was superb. Scholars said his French version of the *Institutes,* finally finished in 1541, had raised the French language to a new level. Once again he paralleled Luther, who everyone agreed had raised German to new heights in his own writing. But John was happy outside his calling, too. His affection for Idelette grew. Soon it was no longer an arrangement but a loving relationship. Nor was John the center of a storm any more. Had God given him peace and prosperity at last? Would he enjoy happy, productive years in relative tranquility like Erasmus had for so many years?

"Perhaps not," he worried, "for once again Geneva beckons."

The city powers in Geneva were not happy with what they thought they wanted: the absence of John and his evangelical colleagues. They had tried to escape moral authority. The church in Geneva was disintegrating. John was repulsed by the thought of returning, writing to a friend, "The thought that chiefly alarms me is what I see when I consider the great gulf into which I should have to enter and which would swallow me up completely."[9]

John felt Geneva would be his martyrdom. Yet he cared for Geneva. When the church of Rome began making overtures about returning to Geneva, the city fathers panicked. "Would John Calvin write the solicitor—Cardinal Jacopo Sadoleto, archbishop of Carpentras—expressing their concern?" they pleaded.

"Although I am for the present relieved of the charge of the Church of Geneva, this circumstance ought not to prevent me from embracing it with paternal affection," he admitted reluctantly in a letter.[10] So John agreed to write the cardinal. He never did anything halfway. John's letter to the cardinal was a masterwork of the lawyer's skills. But its passion transcended legal documents. John cleared the evangelicals of charges of heresy and schism. Moreover, he challenged the cardinal to bring the church of Rome back to the faith of the fathers and apostles of the Church. John's response was certainly not what Rome wanted to hear from Geneva. The councils of Geneva were so impressed by the letter, they printed it and distributed it all over Europe.

"I rejoice that God raises up such men," said Luther after reading the letter.[11]

The fact that Martin Luther himself lauded John's letter certainly enhanced John's reputation with evangelicals. Besides that, it was clear by now that Geneva wanted John back. Two city leaders who had helped oust John and Farel in 1538 had been involved in a nasty brawl during a festival in 1540. One was killed. The second one killed someone else. He was executed. Others in the ouster of John and Farel had also died. Others had left Geneva. It was incredible the way the leaders of the ouster had disappeared. Was it God's judgment? In September 1540, the councils of Geneva officially decided to try to get John back. Order had to be restored. Delegates from Geneva began to contact John. This upset him.

"Tears flowed faster than words," he wrote of one meeting with delegates. Though many thought John was cold, he was in fact a very emotional man. And Geneva triggered his strongest emotions. He was bitter, too. "Rather would I submit to death a hundred times than to that cross on which I had to perish daily a thousand times over," he wrote William Farel.[12]

In yet another letter to Farel he agonized:

Whenever I call to mind the wretchedness of my life there, how can it not be but that my very soul must shudder at any proposal for my return? I will not mention the anxiety by which we were continually tossed up and down and driven to and fro from the time I was appointed your colleague. . . When I remember by what torture my conscience was racked at that time, and with how much anxiety it was continually boiling over, forgive me if I dread the place as having about it something of a fatality in my case. You yourself, with God, are my best witness that no lesser tie could have held me there so long, save that I dared not throw off the yoke of my calling, which I was convinced had been laid on me by the Lord. Therefore, so long as I was bound hand and foot, I preferred to suffer to that extreme rather than for a moment to listen to the thoughts that were apt to come into my mind of moving elsewhere, thoughts which often stole in upon me unawares. But now that by the favor of God I am delivered, who will not excuse me if I am unwilling to plunge again into the gulf and whirlpool which I know to be so dangerous and destructive?[13]

In that letter, John touched on the main criterion for all his decisions. Was it or was it not God's call? No matter how rational his decision making, all logic would be thrown aside in favor of God's will. But this time, John did not have the conviction that he should go to Geneva. On the other hand, he did not have the conviction he should stay in Strasbourg. Why would God not guide John? Geneva kept up the pressure. Could Strasbourg loan John for six months? Strasbourg agreed. This time the Genevans bent over backwards. Wagons were sent to transport John's belongings from his humble quarters in Strasbourg. In September 1541, thirty-two-year-old John Calvin returned to Geneva. He found to his amazement he was being moved into one of the better homes on the rue des Chanoines. It was well furnished. His salary was generous.

"There seems no doubt Geneva really wants us," he bubbled to Idelette.

His first order of business was to establish ecclesiastical ordinances. In his own words, "the Church could not hold together unless a settled government were agreed on, such as is prescribed to us in the Word of God and as was in use in the early Church."[14] The drafting of such rules took a mere two weeks. But then the political process began with the many councils. First came the Little Council, then the Two Hundred, then the General Council. There was only token resistance. John, for the time being at least, had almost a free hand.

However, he did not get his monthly Lord's Supper. They approved only four per year. And there was no prior notification necessary to participate. Every Sunday, howeverthough, sermon services were to be offered at dawn and nine o'clock in the three parish churches: Saint Pierre, La Madeleine, and Saint Gervais. In addition was a three o'clock service in Saint Pierre and Saint Gervais. Children's catechism class was at midday on Sunday in each of the three churches. During the week, more sermons were offered in the three parish churches. This busy schedule was to be carried out by five ministers and three assistants.

"Parishioners are asked to respect parish boundaries," announced John diplomatically.

The church "government" consisted of four orders: pastors, doctors, elders, and deacons. The responsibilities of these orders were to preach the gospel, administer the two sacraments, teach believers the faith, care for the infirm, and exercise discipline. The pastor was primarily to preach, administer sacraments, and to assist in the exercise of discipline. Pastors were elected by the other pastors, then approved by the councils. The pastor took an oath to uphold the ordinances. Internally, the pastors met to study the Bible and critique their performances. With the exception of Pierre Viret, whom John had brought in temporarily, his colleagues were disturbingly mediocre.

John wrote a friend, "Our other colleagues are a hindrance rather than a help to me. They are rude and self-conceited, with no zeal and less learning. Worst of all, I cannot trust them, much as I wish to, for they show their alienation from us in many ways and give hardly any signs of a sincere and trustworthy disposition."[15]

He began to recruit abroad, even imprudently inviting Farel to come. Fortunately Farel refused. John was forced to train the ones he had. Soon he found them passable, although their commitment always fell short of his expectations. The pastor began the church service with a set

157

confession of sin for the whole gathering. He read some appropriate Bible verses, then pronounced absolution: "To all those who in this way repent and seek Jesus Christ for their salvation, I pronounce absolution in the name of the Father, and of the Son, and of the Holy Spirit. Amen."[16] Then the congregation sang the first four commandments. The pastor prayed these laws be "written in our hearts so that we may seek only to serve and obey thee."[17] As the pastor ascended the pulpit, the assembly sang the remaining six commandments. At the pulpit, the pastor recited a set prayer, followed by the Lord's Prayer. Next, the congregation sang a psalm, and the pastor prayed an improvised prayer. Only then did the pastor deliver the sermon. The sermon was the bulk of the service, all the rest of the service taking a mere fifteen minutes. After the sermon came a few short prayers and one more song.

In his very first sermon in Geneva in 1541, the meticulous John picked up from his last sermon in Geneva in 1538! "By which I indicated," he noted, "that I had interrupted my office of preaching for a time rather than that I had given it up entirely."[18]

John himself was now a polished preacher. No preacher was more aware of why he preached than John. Preaching was always exposition of the Word of God. Preaching was always grounded in Scriptures. John so revered the church fathers, he followed their practice of preaching without break through whole books of the Bible, even if it took many Sunday sermons. For the sermon, John had at hand both the Old Testament in Hebrew and New Testament in Greek. He preached without notes, but he resented any notion he was unprepared.

He explained:

> *If I should enter the pulpit without deigning to glance at a book, and should frivolously think to myself, "Oh well, when I preach, God will give me enough to say," and come here without troubling to read or thinking what I ought to declare, and do not carefully consider how I must apply Holy Scripture to the edification of the people, then I should be an arrogant upstart. . . .*[19]

He was highly animated when preaching. He could scold, invite to intimacy, rant, and patiently explain. He could enact scenes. "Ho! you can't tell me what to do," he protested rebelliously, acting the sinner in one scene. Then he assumed the role of a calm mentor, "My friend, what you are really saying is that you do not want God to reign over you, and you want to abolish the law."[20] In another scene John as the sinner shouted, "We want to be taught differently from this!" This time a not-so-calm mentor, John shouted back, "Well then, go to the devil's school; he will flatter you well enough to your destruction."[22] Depicting John as a stern, humorless taskmaster before a cowering assembly was woefully inaccurate. His congregation clamored for John to take more sermons than he did.

But I have so many other duties, he thought to himself.

John was also a "doctor" of the church. Another of the four orders of the churches in Geneva, the doctors instructed believers in true doctrine and expunged errors. For biblical studies, two professors taught the Old and New Testaments. In addition, a schoolmaster and assistants taught the humanities and the languages. Because these doctors also administered the boys' school and a separate girls' school. Naturally if a pastor possessed great formal training, as John did, he was included also among the doctors of the church.

The elders, a third order of the church, were twelve laypeople from the councils. The elders combined with the pastors to form the consistory. The consistory met every Thursday to administer discipline. Because the laypeople far outnumbered the pastors on the consistory, it was thought this would prevent too much zeal against sinners. Offenders, for offenses as minor as not attending service or as major as adultery, were called before the consistory to be admonished. Repentance usually brought no more than a scolding. Defiance or a repeated offense resulted in no access to the Lord's Supper. More than three admonitions brought excommunication. The consistory had no other power to punish. If any offense seemed to merit more punishment, they had to turn the matter over to the civil authority of the councils.

The consistory constantly reminded itself that admonitions were "only medicines for bringing back sinners to our Lord."[23] They were not to drive people away from the church.

The deacons, the fourth order, were members of the church who helped the other orders in various capacities. However, they were largely responsible for distributing relief to the poor and the sick. It seemed a narrow responsibility, but in those days it was a very large, very tiring task. Even in a commercial city like Geneva poverty was widespread. Disease was rampant, too, and the dreaded plague still a frequent visitor.

For his own roles as pastor and doctor, John reproved himself. He was conscious of the perception he was stern and unforgiving. He tried very hard to be amiable and compassionate. During the first months at Geneva he wrote a friend:

> *They all know by experience the pleasant and human character of Viret. I am in no way more harsh, at any rate in this matter. Perhaps you will hardly believe this, but it is true all the same. I value the public peace and hearty concord among ourselves so highly that I restrain myself. Even our opponents have to give me this credit. And this feeling prevails to such an extent that day by day those who were once open enemies have become friends. Others I conciliate by courtesy, and I feel that I have been successful in some measure—although not everywhere and always. . . .*[24]

Although many in the future would remember the strict enforcement of morality at Geneva and credit all that to John, his primary duties were pastoring and teaching. And the discipline that was enforced was aimed to accentuate the learning of the gospel and participating in the sacraments. John alone performed about thirty weddings and five baptisms a year, in addition to delivering hundreds of sermons and visiting the sick or those in prison.

twelve

During 1542, the churches in Geneva introduced their own service book. It detailed instructions for the prayers, sacraments, and rites. It also contained the songs of the church. To John, singing was "like a spur to incite us to pray to and to praise God, to meditate on His works, that we may love, fear, honor, and glorify Him."[1] Like many others, John Calvin insisted psalms made the best songs because they were composed by the Holy Spirit. Yet as much as John loved the psalms, he was willing to add contemporary hymns. He particularly favored those of Clément Marot and Louis Bourgeois. This joyous singing was often forgotten or ignored by later critics who characterized the service as stern and glum. The truth was otherwise.

John wrote, "Among other things which recreate man and give him pleasure, music is either the first or at least

162

one of the principal; and we should reckon it a gift of God intended for this use."[2]

The year 1542 brought a dreaded visitor to Geneva: the plague!

The outbreak of the plague accentuated the weakness of John's fellow pastors. The worthy Viret, as agreed, had returned to Bern after six months. John himself had abandoned the idea of returning to Strasbourg. There was too much to do. Of the other pastors only one, Pierre Blanchet, would visit the plague wards. The others had so little trust in God they refused. The year was particularly painful to John anyway. When his wife Idelette gave birth to a baby boy, baptized James, the tiny infant lingered only a few days and died.

"The Lord has certainly inflicted a severe and bitter wound in the death of our baby son," John wrote a friend. "But He is Himself a father, and knows best what is good for His children."[3]

To make matters worse, Idelette could not seem to recover her health. In subsequent letters to his friends, John often noted that Idelette was sick in bed. In spite of John's excellent home, he lived very frugally. His house and furniture actually belonged to the councils. Because of his location in a wealthy neighborhood, once in a while his enemies would start rumors he was living like a king.

"I am still using someone else's furniture," he fumed. "Neither the table at which we eat, nor the bed on which we sleep, is my own."[4]

Nevertheless the house was large. Idelette's daughter still lived with them. And so did brother Antoine with his wife and children. There were still more rooms for servants and guests. And the location served him well for his circle of friends. His old friend Nicolas Cop lived nearby, as did other notable scholars and evangelicals like his old mentor at the Collège de la Marche, distinguished Latinist Mathurin Cordier. But home was no leisurely refuge for John. Besides administering a very large household, he conducted endless pastoral duties there, too.

His contemporary Nicolas Colladon wrote:

> *Who could recount his ordinary and extraordinary labors? I doubt if any man in our time has had more to listen to, to reply to, to write, or things of greater importance. The multitude and quality alone of his writings are enough to astonish everyone who looks at them, and even more those who read them. . . He never ceased working, day and night, in the service of the Lord, and heard most unwillingly the prayers and exhortations that his friends addressed to him every day to give himself some rest. . . .*[5]

Once John complained in a letter, "The difficulty arises from the annoyances and interruptions of the train of thought which intervene to break off a letter in the midst twenty times over, or even more, beyond all bounds. . . ."[6]

Colladon described more of John's personal traits:

> *As to his ordinary life, everyone will bear witness that he was very abstemious, without any excess or meanness, but a praiseworthy moderation. It is true that for his stomach's sake he abstained from some*

*common foods that he was fond of, but this was
without being fastidious or troublesome in company.
One fault he had was that in his abstinence he took
little regard to his health, mostly being content for
many years with a single meal a day and never taking anything between two meals. . . His reasons
were the weakness of his stomach and his migraine,
which he said he had proved by experiment could be
remedied only by a continual diet. Sometimes I have
known him go without any food into the second day.*[7]

John took care of his health, but in no way did he ever
encourage ascetic self-torture. He felt that asceticism was
like praying loudly in the square, a show for other men.
But John was frail, as Colladon noted in describing John's
peculiar ways of working:

*Being so frail he also slept very little; but for
all the lassitude that ensued from this he never
failed to be ready for his work and the exercises of
his office. When it was not his turn to preach, he
had books brought to him in bed at five or six
o'clock, so that he might compose, having someone to write for him. If it was his week, he was
always ready at the hour to go into the pulpit;
then afterwards at home he lay down on the bed
fully clothed and pursued his labors on some
book. . . This is how in the mornings he dictated
the most of his books, when he could give his
genius full flow. While the dictating was going on,
someone would be sure to call and perhaps stay*

for half an hour or even an hour. But then usually
he remembered the connection where he had
stopped and went on with what he had been say-
ing without being reminded. . . .[8]

John also maintained a vast correspondence. Of course he regularly wrote his great friend Farel in Neuchâatel. He wrote Henry Bullinger, Zwingli's successor in Zurich. He exchanged many letters with his colleague Pierre Viret. He wrote Bucer in Strasbourg. He wrote many colleagues in England, including King Edward VI, Henry VIII's son and successor, and Thomas Cranmer, archbishop of Canterbury and promoter of a Bible in English. He wrote the King of Poland. He wrote John Knox, the evangelical leader in Scotland. John sent letters all over Europe to bolster those who were being persecuted. He corresponded with prisoners. He regularly wrote his old friend Renee, duchess of Ferrara, whom he had convinced to convert in 1540. She was under constant pressure from her husband to renounce evangelicalism.

The results of his correspondence were not always agreeable. His 1545 letter to Luther in Wittenberg, accompanied by some of John's writings, dripped with praise for the old Reformer:

To the very excellent pastor of the Christian
Church, Dr. M. Luther, my much respected father.
In two little tractates, wherein, if it shall not
be troublesome to you to glance over them, you
will more clearly perceive both what I think, and
the reasons which have compelled me to form that

opinion. . . [but some] are desirous to hear your opinion, which as they do deservedly hold in reverence, so it shall serve greatly to confirm them. They have therefore requested me, that I would undertake to send a trusty messenger to you, who might report your answer to us upon this question . . . Now, therefore, much respected father in the Lord, I beseech you by Christ, that you will not grudge to take the trouble for their sake and mine, first, that you would peruse the epistle written in their name, and my little books, cursorily and at leisure hours. . . [and] that you would write back your opinion in a few words. . .

. . . Adieu, most renowned Sir, most distinguished minister of Christ, and my ever-honored father. The Lord Himself rule and direct you by His own Spirit, that you may persevere even unto the end, for the common benefit and good of His own Church.[9]

John was astonished by the reply from Wittenberg. It was not from Luther but his right-hand man Melanchthon:

I have not shown your letter to Dr. Martin, for he takes up many things suspiciously, and does not like his replies to questions of the kind you have proposed to him, to be carried round and handed from one to another. . .[10]

John was rankled by the tone of the response and subsequent reports that Luther was attacking the Swiss Reformers again in print. Never again would he write Luther, but he did reply to Melanchthon in 1545:

> *[Luther] allows himself to be carried beyond all due bounds with his love of thunder, especially seeing that his own case is by no means the better of the two. We all of us do acknowledge that we are much indebted to him. Neither shall I submit myself unwillingly, but be quite content, that he may bear the chief sway, provided that he can manage to conduct himself with moderation. Howbeit, in the Church we must always be upon our guard, lest we pay too great a deference to men. For it is all over with her, when a single individual, be he whosoever you please, has more authority than all the rest, especially where this very person does not scruple to try how far he may go. . . But, you will say, his disposition is vehement, and his impetuosity is ungovernable—as if that very vehemence did not break forth with all the greater violence when all show themselves alike indulgent to him, and allow him to have his way, unquestioned. If this specimen of overbearing tyranny has sprung forth already as the early blossom in the spring-tide of a reviving Church, what must we expect in a short time. . . Let us therefore bewail the calamity of the Church. . . .*[11]

John's angry reply was unwise. His response was triggered by pride. And enemies of evangelicalism used the quarrel as ammunition against the Reform. In addition, he caused grief to Melanchthon, a sympathetic friend. And lastly, within a year of this futile correspondence, John would learn the volatile Luther was dead. He would learn that Luther had severe health problems, not the least of which were excruciating bouts with kidney stones. Many days Luther would bloat grotesquely and not function at all. Later in his life, John would himself experience the battles with "stones," too painful to contemplate and too degrading in their nature to speak of. So John forgave Luther his hot temper and impatience with inquirers. And John had to ask God for forgiveness in indulging his anger against Luther and Melanchthon.

But perhaps John could be forgiven for his own temper in those days. Because even though he was supported by the councils, he and his temperate influence were increasingly opposed by many others in Geneva. Some later historians would dwell only on this strife, but from John's viewpoint the opposition was merely another nuisance that hindered his main work for Christ. Nevertheless, opposition was real. Some of it was manifested as vicious gossip. For example, a woman found out that Idelette and her first husband had been married in the Anabaptist church and not by a magistrate. So she sullied Idelette's reputation. The unprincipled woman represented no faction of religious opposition but only those wanting license to sin. They feared John and his colleagues might take away their wine and ale and more. So far the consistory had only tried to clean up the taverns, banning swearing, slandering, and dancing—even insisting the owner keep a French Bible on the premises. Still, this was enough of a threat to prompt many of this base element to constantly slur the evangelicals.

"But they are not the great danger to the church," assessed John calmly.

The real danger came from politicians who wanted to subdue the church. In 1543, a powerful secular member in the consistory insisted only the councils had the right to excommunicate. John threatened to leave Geneva if that happened. So the opposition backed off for the time being. By 1545, the opposing politicians began to really organize. They were angered by a mandate to attend church and by the discipline administered on sinners. They were determined to lessen the influence of the church. Though they were wealthy people, their behavior was often juvenile. One man named Berthelier made it a habit to cough violently during John's sermons.

When John complained to the consistory the man whined, "Why am I being persecuted for being ill?"

Yet there were irritating extremes in the church's administration of discipline. Through the consistory they even tried to regulate the naming of children. John himself was drawn into that silliness. Only certain names, preferably from the Old Testament, were acceptable for Christening. Names of Catholic saints were forbidden.

Once in the pulpit of Saint Pierre John found a note:

> *Big pot-belly, you and your fellows would do better to shut up. If you drive us too far, you will find yourselves in a situation where you will curse the day you skipped your monastery. We've had enough of blaming people. Why the devil have these [word deleted] renegade priests come here to ruin us? Those who have had enough take their*

*revenge. Beware that you don't get what happened
to Monsieur Werly of Fribourg. We don't want all
these masters. Beware of what I say.*[12]

Werly had been murdered in 1533 by his opposition.
So John was concerned. This threat to John went beyond
juvenile harassment. Later a letter of the wealthy Jacques
Gruet was confiscated that read, "Do not be ruled by the
voice or the will of one man. . . often the opinion of one
single man will cause much evil. . . he will hate everything
contrary to his nature. . . suppose I am a man who wants to
eat his meals as he pleases, what affair is that of others? Or
if I want to dance, or have a good time, what is that to do
with the law? Nothing."[13] This seemed a mild rebellion, but
was Gruet behind the death threat?

To the discredit of the Reformers, they condoned the
torture of Gruet until he confessed to a number of plots to
harm the church and even actual crimes. Some of the
crimes required the death penalty. And indeed Gruet was
beheaded in July 1546. In the macabre logic of that age,
beheading was considered more merciful than burning.
Fortunately for John's conscience, the subsequent discov-
ery of a notebook confirmed that Gruet was pathological in
his hatred of Christ and the church.

"Gruet actually confessed to fewer crimes than he had
committed," relieved evangelicals informed John.

Had John ever anticipated that strict enforcement of
discipline would result in executions? He wanted to spread
the gospel, not become an executioner. Yet the execution
was widely supported. Bucer in Strasbourg approved the
death penalty for blasphemy or heresy. Bullinger in Zurich

agreed. The Germans also approved. Even more than the Swiss, the Germans executed religious rivals as heretics, especially Anabaptists. In 1536, Melanchthon had drafted a memorandum that Luther signed recommending death for public *or private* practice of Anabaptism. It should be noted this lethal attitude toward heretics was not punishment invented by evangelicals in the sixteenth century. They were continuing the kind of totalitarian discipline long practiced by the church of Rome against heretics.

Yet John himself did not demur. He approved the death penalty for heretics. There was no ambivalence in his attitude. Heresy was a crime against Christ. Moreover, protesting punishment made one an accomplice! He wrote:

> *Whoever shall maintain that wrong is done to heretics and blasphemers in punishing them makes himself an accomplice in their crime. . . There is no question here of man's authority; it is God who speaks, and it is clear what law He would have kept in the Church even to the end of the world. Wherefore does He demand of us so extreme severity if not to show us that due honor is not paid Him so long as we set not His service above every human consideration, so that we spare not kin nor blood of any, and forget all humanity when the matter is to combat for His glory. . .[14]*

John's most powerful enemy in Geneva became Ami Perrin, a member of the councils and the consistory. His opposition had surfaced in 1545 when he and his wife were disciplined for their lewd behavior at a party. Perrin denied the accusations. But there were many witnesses. John wrote to him: that "I will not be moved from asserting it [the law of my heavenly Master] with a good conscience for the sake of any man living."[15] Perrin's wife became hostile, too.

She happily gossiped, "Pestilences run in seven-year cycles and John Calvin has almost reached the end of his blight on Geneva!"

By 1548, Perrin gained real influence in the consistory. He regularly ranted against John. The fiery Farel happened to be present at one meeting and defended John in a fury. But there were more and more stormy meetings. And John's opponents continued to grow in influence on the consistory. In 1547 King Francis I died. Perrin, representing the councils, rushed to France to pay the respects of Geneva. On his return, he was accused of plotting with the French against the city-state of Geneva. This was not unreasonable because the evangelicals knew the new French king, Henry II, was rabidly Catholic and planned to purge France of evangelicals. The charge against Perrin could not be proven, but Perrin was stripped of his important position.

Perrin's supporters fulminated a riot, as John described in a letter to Viret:

> *Much confused shouting was heard from that quarter [the council chamber]. This got so loud that there was surely a riot. I at once run up to the place. Everything looks terrible. I throw myself into the thickest of the crowds, to the amazement of everyone. The whole mob makes a rush towards me; they seize me and drag me hither and thither—no doubt lest I*

should be injured! I called God and men to witness
that I had come to present my body to their swords. I
bade them, if they wanted to shed blood, to start with
me. Even the worthless, but especially the more
respectable, at once cooled down. I was at length
dragged through the midst of them to the Council.
There new fights started, and I threw myself between
them. . . I succeeded in getting everyone to sit down
quietly, and then delivered a long and vehement
speech, which they say moved all of them.[16]

This may have seemed a triumph for John who had
often lost control in public disputes, but he was very disturbed by the incident. Always frail and reed-thin he began
to deteriorate. He wrote in 1546:

Although I am pretty well physically, I am
unceasingly tormented with a heaviness which
will not let me do a thing. Apart from the sermons
and lectures, there is a month gone by in which I
have scarce done anything, in such wise that I am
almost ashamed to live thus useless.[17]

Questionable health or not, he certainly had no desire
to throw himself into any more mobs. "I have not yet
decided what I am going to do, except that I can no longer
tolerate the ways of this people," he confided to friends in
a moment of doubt.[18]

His opposition were now formally called the Libertines.
The meaning was ambiguous. Members insisted it meant
"freedom." Others insisted it meant "freedom to sin." The

174

next incident with a Libertine involved Roux Monet, a young man charged with possessing and promoting pornography. He also was rumored to have committed adultery with no less than four wives of council members, including the wife of Perrin! His defense was hopeless considering the law and who was administering the law. He had offended the very councils that judged him. Perrin had been a friend, but now even he stepped aside as Monet was convicted and executed.

By 1549 John Calvin was an old forty, the veteran of constant strife and stress. Erasmus was dead. As was Zwingli. Luther was dead. So was Henry VIII. Francis I was dead, as was his wonderful sister Marguerite. John was beginning to feel ancient, his physical ailments and pains more and more nagging. To afflict him most of all was the condition of Idelette. Her health was becoming hopeless. She had been sick for months in 1545. Then she failed again in 1547, only to get worse in 1548. By early 1549, everyone including John and Idelette herself knew she was dying.

When John began to bring up the subject of the children with the dying Idelette, she had said, "I have already committed them to God."[19]

John assured her he would not neglect them.

"I know you will not neglect what you know has been committed to God," she replied.

On the day she died she suddenly gasped in short bursts, "Oh glorious resurrection! Oh God of Abraham and of all our fathers, in thee have the faithful trusted during so many past ages, and none of them have trusted in vain. I also will hope."[20]

Within two hours she was dead, having passed away

"so calmly, that those present could scarcely distinguish between her life and her death."[21]

On April 7, 1549, John wrote Viret of those last days:

> *Although the death of my wife has been exceedingly painful to me, yet I subdue my grief as well as I can. . . you know well enough how tender, or rather soft, my mind is. Had not a powerful self-control, therefore, been vouchsafed to me, I could not have borne up so long. And truly mine is no common source of grief. I have been bereaved of the best companion of my life, of one who, had it been so ordered, would not only have been the willing sharer of my indigence, but even of my death. During her life she was the faithful helper of my ministry. From her I never experienced the slightest hindrance. She was never troublesome to me through-out the entire course of her illness; she was more anxious about her children than about herself. . . .*[22]

Viret replied:

> *Numerous messengers. . . have informed me how you, with a heart so broken and lacerated, have attended to all your duties even better than hitherto. . . Go on then as you have begun. . . and I pray God most earnestly that you may be enabled to do so, and that you may receive daily greater comfort and be strengthened more and more. . . .*[23]

Could John, worn-out and heart-broken, persevere?

thirteen

John did persevere, but the atmosphere in the Calvin household was grim. John was in mourning, and his brother Antoine had his own problems. His wife had been accused of adultery in 1548, but proof was not conclusive. Yet John suspected she was still misbehaving. John lost himself in his work. His chief writing was his constant revision of the *Institutes*—he had yet another revision printed in 1550—and his continual work on commentaries.

"God willing it, I intend to write a commentary on every book in the Bible," he vowed.

He had started with a commentary on the Book of Romans in 1540. By 1550, he had added commentaries on Paul's epistles to Corinthians, Galatians, Ephesians, Philippians, Colossians, Timothy, Titus, and probably Thessalonians. He had also done Hebrews and Jude. The dates of

Matthew, Luke, and John, and Acts are uncertain, but probably they were done after 1550. Many of these were simultaneous works in progress. Aides worked on some, patching in John's sermons. So the commentaries were uneven in style and quality. In the New Testament, John planned to do the difficult Book of Revelation last. In the Old Testament, John started with the three most important sections for Christians: the Pentateuch (first five books including Genesis), Isaiah, and the Psalms.

In conjunction with writing commentaries, he taught on the same subjects. In contrast to his preaching style, his lecturing style was very subdued and unadorned. Later writers characterized his lecturing as "rather in the old-fashioned, pre-Renaissance manner," "more in the scholastic than in the oratorical style," in a "simple though not uncultured mode of speaking," "much like that which was used in lectures in former days."[1] John would dryly read the Bible in its original language, then translate the passage into Latin.

"French will be of no use in John Calvin's lectures," noted students.

A student named Jacques Bourgouin sketched John while he lectured. Wearing the high fur collar of the day, John appeared to have no neck. His flat-topped, ear-flapped headgear shortened his forehead. Because in addition he had a mustache and long thick beard, his face seemed but a long thin pointed nose and piercing eyes. Bourgouin's black ink sketches captured a man who was humorless and driven. God may have been sovereign, but John Calvin was one of his most obsessed earthly messengers. Earlier portraits prove he had looked that same way since he had reached manhood.

"It is a severe, no-nonsense look he intentionally conveys," realized Bourgouin.

Of course, John delivered far more sermons than lectures—and not dryly but in his highly animated style. He had a habit of preaching the Old Testament on weekdays and the New Testament on Sundays. Sometimes, however, he preached from Psalms on Sunday afternoons. Little is known of the specific books he preached on before 1549. One could surmise he preached much on Paul's epistles, because they are the books he interpreted in his commentaries during that time. From 1549 on, a local society tried very diligently to write down his sermons and transcribe them for permanent records. This was possible only because they found Denis Raguenier, a man who was a marvel at "shorthand," a system possibly of his own invention.

Because of Raguenier, John's sermons for the next fourteen years are known in great detail. From the Old Testament, he preached from Jeremiah and Lamentations during 1550, from the Minor Prophets and Daniel during 1550 to 1552, from Ezekiel during 1552 to 1554, from Job during 1554 and 1555, from Deuteronomy during 1555 to 1556, from Isaiah during 1556 to 1559, from Genesis during 1559 to 1561, from Judges during 1561, from 1 and 2 Samuel during 1561 to 1563 and from 1 Kings during 1563 to 1564. From 1549 to 1564, John moved through the New Testament in the following order: Acts, some of the remaining Pauline epistles, then the Gospels.

"How I relish lecturing, preaching, and writing," he admitted to himself.

Yet—like Luther before him—John seldom could relish

these moments of joy for long. Small problems abounded daily. Major problems popped up every year or so. In 1551, John had to deal with controversy around Jerome Bolsec. Bolsec was a refugee from Paris, an evangelical and a physician. Like many others he was enraged by John's interpretation of the Bible on "double predestination." Specifically John had written in the *Institutes*:

> *We call predestination God's eternal decree,
> by which He determined with Himself what He
> willed to become of each man. For all are not cre-
> ated in equal condition; rather, eternal life is fore-
> ordained for some, eternal damnation for others.
> Therefore, as any man has been created to one or
> the other of these ends, we speak of Him as pre-
> destined to life or death.*[2]

How some people hated this doctrine! It seemed so unfair. Bolsec was one of them. In a public forum, he insisted that election and non-election were not eternal decrees of God but dependent on the faith of the individual. He further declared that double predestination was not a doctrine of Augustine's. This was absurd. Few scholars knew Augustine's works better than John, who had incorporated even more of Augustine in his 1550 revision of the *Institutes*. Bolsec claimed the doctrine of predestination was not in the Bible. People like John had distorted the Scriptures to try to prove the doctrine.

"Those who posit an eternal decree in God by which He has ordained some to life and the rest to death," cried

Bolsec, "make of Him a tyrant, and in fact an idol, as the pagans made of Jupiter."[3]

That angry remark about making God an idol was a mistake. It was slanderous under Genevan laws. Bolsec was arrested. The civil court tried Bolsec because he had broken a law of Geneva. The trial became a theological debate. Bolsec was woefully prepared for such an event. He had no chance against John and other church theologians. He was convicted of breaking the law. In an odd turn the court, perhaps prompted by the Libertines, solicited opinions from churches in three other cities. Neuchâaatel, influenced by Farel, sided strongly with John's argument. Basel agreed with John but made a much milder argument than John had. Zurich also fell short of John's argument. Fortunately, Geneva showed Bolsec mercy. He was merely banished from Geneva.

In 1552, the Libertines made strong gains in the councils. Even Berthelier, the lout who disrupted John's sermons with his fake coughing, gained an important position. Berthelier and his like were brazen, openly taunting pastors in the street. By 1553, they demanded from the pastors a list of everyone who had been excommunicated and the reasons why. Some members of the councils had long wanted to be in complete control of who was excommunicated. That way the Libertines could protect their own miscreants. Again John and his colleagues refused. In anger John tried to resign. His tormentors backed off.

"We want the satisfaction of a groveling, whipped Calvin," they chortled secretly, "not a saint battling us from Strasbourg or Basel."

By 1553, John very nearly became a groveling, whipped man. In August of that year Michael Servetus, a fugitive from southern France, arrived in Geneva. John had known about Servetus since the 1530s in Paris. Servetus was a physician from Spain and somewhat of a genius, who had discovered the role of the lungs in circulating blood. But his radical views on the Trinity always had him in trouble with authorities, both Catholic and evangelical. He did not deny the Trinity but redefined it. To Servetus, the "Son of God" was the peculiar union of the eternal Word with the man Jesus. John had corresponded with Servetus over the years, always in heated arguments.

Once John wrote Farel:

> *Servetus lately wrote to me and coupled with his letter a long volume of his delirious fancies. . . He would like to come here if it is agreeable to me. But I do not wish to pledge my word for his safety. For, if he comes, I will never let him depart alive, if I have any authority.[4]*

It was clear John believed Servetus a heretic who deserved death! And in 1553 someone recognized Servetus in Geneva, and he was jailed. Then the councils tried him as a heretic. John and his Genevan evangelicals appeared as his accusers. Enmeshed in the trial were the Libertines on the councils, who intended to drag it out as much as possible to embarrass John and the evangelicals. Servetus assumed the Libertines were going to protect him and became as obnoxious as possible to John. The Libertines were delighted.

However, someone found out that Servetus had escaped jail in southern France. He had been arrested for heresy there, too. With the assent of the other Reformed churches in Switzerland, the councils made it appear that they were only carrying out the sentence of that jurisdiction in southern France: death by burning. John did nothing to intervene except ask that Servetus be spared burning. John recommended beheading. But the Genevans burned Servetus.

John's views on punishing heretics had not changed since his first edition of *Institutes* in 1536. It was the duty of the civil government to prevent the dissemination of false doctrines. Authorities must weigh the death of the heretic against the losses of souls that would be caused by the heretic. But the evangelicals and their governments were not consistent. Basel had tolerated Servetus at one time, but the Genevans put him to death. On the other hand, the Genevans had long tolerated a heretic named Valentin Gentile, but in 1566 the Bernese executed him for the same views.

The calm way Geneva citizens accepted the result of the Servetus trial surprised the Libertines. They expected public outrage. February 1554 brought the Libertines an even greater surprise. Nearly every one lost in the elections to the councils. Suddenly John's antagonists were out of power. And he was strong again. The Libertines then fell victim to their own indulgent ways. Perrin, Berthelier, and others goaded each other into a frenzy while drinking in a tavern. Drunk and angry they tried to burn down a house of their enemies. Many members of the councils witnessed their murderous behavior. Once sober, Perrin and his cohorts fled Geneva. In their absence they were convicted and sentenced to death by the councils.

"At least they can never return," rationalized the evangelicals.

John's home life was still full of pain, though. He was not going to remarry. Surely he felt no one could live up to his memory of Idelette, but he had other reasons, too. Once in a sermon he was very candid:

> *As for me, I do not want anyone to think me very virtuous because I am not married. It would rather be a fault in me if I could serve God better in marriage than remaining as I am. . . But I know my infirmity, that perhaps a woman might not be happy with me. However that may be, I abstain from marriage in order that I may be more free to serve God. But this is not because I think that I am more virtuous than my brethren. Fie to me if I had that false opinion![4]*

It is not clear what his infirmity was. He had many illnesses. But it is likely he referred to his frequent bad temper. His own family certainly intruded its problems into his life. Antoine's first wife, often suspected, had finally been caught in adultery with a servant. In 1557 she was banished from Geneva. To make matters worse, John learned that the servant had been stealing from the household. Then his stepdaughter, the daughter of his precious Idelette, delivered a hammer blow to John. She, too, was caught in adultery. "I know you will not neglect what you know has been committed to God," the dying Idelette had said.[5] Oh, how he had betrayed his dear wife's trust.

"For surely I have had neglected my stepdaughter," he cried.

John withdrew into himself. Then the situation worsened. It became public. "The great moralizer can not even manage his own household," snickered his detractors. For days John could not leave that household to face the public.

fourteen

Yet John Calvin recovered. He had too much to do to wallow in shame and self-pity. Over the next years John preached, wrote, and taught. The evangelicals, long champions of public education, now established a university at Geneva. Instrumental in its founding were Theodore Beza and the influx of top teachers from Lausanne. The university made theology the ultimate achievement in education. The arts and sciences were mere preparation. But John's heart was in revising the *Institutes* and adding new commentaries. He spent his time on the Old Testament. With the exception of Revelation, John had finished the New Testament. Perhaps, like Luther, he regarded Revelation as too obscure.

"A revelation should be revealing," Luther had blustered in frustration.[1]

John's health was so bad by this time, he knew his revision of the *Institutes* would be his last. He expanded much of it as well as modified and clarified the rest. As an example of how the work had mushroomed, one needed only to trace the history of chapter six—titled "On Christian Liberty"—since the first edition. In the second edition, he made that chapter's three topics—Christian liberty itself, the authority of the Church, and civil government—three separate chapters. In the 1543 edition, he dispersed those three chapters in a different structure. In 1559, although he only modified the topics of Christian liberty and civil government, he expanded the topic of the authority of the church into twelve chapters!

His writing reached its zenith in style in the Latin edition in 1559. But the French version he finished in 1560 was flawed. John's health had deteriorated, and he rushed the translation. Antoine and his helpers were often unable to follow his instructions. Beza was brought in to try to straighten it out. The result was so muddled that years later scholars believed the French work was not that of John Calvin at all. But the Latin edition became a standard for evangelicals of various persuasions who now completely dominated Switzerland, England, Scotland, and Scandinavia. They vied for dominance with Catholicism in France, Germany, Poland, and Holland. Only Ireland, Italy, and Spain remained solidly Catholic. That situation, already established by 1560, would persist for centuries.

But the situation was not static. Struggles went on. John especially regretted not being able to help the French evangelicals called "Huguenots." Many atrocities had been committed against them. And the killings continued. Nor could he help his convert Renee of Ferrara. Her life was misery. Her husband the duke had taken her children from her. She had been imprisoned for a while in 1554. Finally in 1560, she had fled to an evangelical stronghold in France, where she remained an active witness. But her children were so alienated from her, they condemned her. Renee had paid a heavy price for her loyalty to Christ.

John summed up his own condition in a letter of 1564:

Twenty years ago. . . I was not attacked by arthritic pains, knew nothing of the stone or the gravel—I was not tormented with the gripings of the cholic, nor afflicted with hemorrhoids, nor threatened with expectoration of blood. At present all these ailments as it were in troops assail me. As soon as I recovered from a. . . [fever in 1558], I was seized with severe and acute pains in the calves of my legs, which after being partially relieved returned a second and a third time. At last they degenerated into a disease in my articulations, which spread from my feet to my knees. An ulcer in the hemorrhoid veins long caused me excruciating sufferings, and intestinal ascarides [worms] subjected me to painful titillations, though I am now relieved from this vermicular [worm-caused] disease, but immediately after in the course of last summer I had an attack of nephritis. . . to my surprise I discovered that I discharged blood instead of urine. As soon as I got

*home I took to bed. The nephritis gave me exquis-
ite pain. . . My sedentary way of life to which I am
condemned by the gout in my feet precludes all
hopes of a cure. . . But I am thoughtlessly tasking
your patience. . . [with] my vain complaints. . . .[2]*

His condition, as he expected, worsened. Weeks later
he wrote Bullinger in Zurich:

*Although the pain in my side is abated, my
lungs are so full of phlegm that my breathing is difficult and short. A stone in my bladder has been
very troublesome for the last twelve days. Add to
that our anxiety. For all remedies have so far
proved ineffectual. Horseriding would have been
best, but an ulcer in the hemorrhoid veins tortures
me even when sitting down or lying in bed, so that I
could not bear the agitation of riding. Within the
last three days, the gout has also been very troublesome. You will not be surprised, then, if so many
sufferings make me lazy. I can hardly be brought to
take any food. The taste of wine is bitter.[3]*

Yes, his life then was bitter. Days later, in April 1564,
John made out his will. He owned almost nothing. He left
small amounts of money to the college, a charitable orga-
nization, his sister Maria's daughter, and brother Antoine's
children. In early May, he bid William Farel adieu in a letter, ending it, "Since it is God's will that you should out-
live me, remember our friendship. It was useful to God's

Church, and its fruits await us in heaven. I do not want you to tire yourself on my account. I draw my breath with difficulty and expect each moment to breathe my last. It is enough that I live and die for Christ, who is to all His followers a gain both in life and in death."[4]

And yet William Farel, seventy-five years old but ever independent, came from Neuchâatel to see John anyway. Council members also visited John's home. He asked their forgiveness for not accomplishing enough. He also asked them to forgive his bad temper and short patience, habits that shamed him. The members returned the following day. John was now sure he was dying. He was having a problem breathing. He often fainted.

He had a grim message. "I am quite different from other sick people," he told them. "When they come near to their end, their senses fail and they become delirious. I certainly feel stupefied, but it seems as if God wants to concentrate all my inward senses. I believe I shall have much difficulty, and that it will cost me a great effort to die."[5]

He then reminisced at length. "When I first came to this Church, I found almost nothing in it. There was preaching and that was all. They would look out for idols, it is true, and burn them. But there was no reformation; everything was in disorder. . . I have lived here amid continual strifes. I have been saluted in derision of an evening before my door with forty or fifty arquebus [musket] shots. Just imagine how that frightened a poor scholar, timid as I am, and as I confess I have always been.

"Then afterwards I was expelled from this city and went to Strasbourg; and when I had lived there some time

I was called back here. But I had no less trouble when I tried to do my duty than previously. They set the dogs at my heels, calling out 'Wretch! Wretch!', and they snapped at my gown and my legs. . . though I am nothing, yet I well know that I have prevented three thousand tumults that might have broken out in Geneva. But take courage and fortify yourselves, for God will make use of this church and will maintain it and assures you that He will protect it.

"I have had many infirmities which you have been obliged to bear with, and what is more, all I have done has been worth nothing. The ungodly will greedily seize upon this word, but I say it again that all I have done has been worth nothing, and that I am a miserable creature. But certainly I can say this, that. . . that my vices have always displeased me, and that the root of the fear of God has been in my heart; and you may say that the disposition was good; and I pray you, that the evil be forgiven me, and if there was any good, that you conform yourselves to it and make it an example.

"As to my doctrine, I have taught faithfully, and God has given me grace to write what I have written as faithfully as it was in my power. I have not falsified a single passage of the Scriptures, nor given it a wrong interpretation to the best of my knowledge; and though I might have introduced subtle senses, had I studied subtlety, I cast that temptation under my feet and always aimed at simplicity.

"I have written nothing out of hatred to any one, but I have always faithfully propounded what I esteemed to be for the glory of God. . . ."[6]

John, not yet fifty-five years old, did die hard. It was

191

not until May 27, 1564, that the councils recorded: "Today about eight o'clock in the evening. . . John Calvin has gone to God whole and entire in sense and understanding, thanks be to God."[7]

The next day, according to his wish, he was buried in the common cemetery with no head marker.

fifteen

Retrospect

After John's death, his own followers still argued over election and predestination. God's election of both the saved and the damned just didn't seem fair to some. Moreover, many could not reconcile that conclusion with free will. Did not believers or non-believers have any influence on their own salvation? Within decades of John's death, opposition to strict "Calvinism" grew up around the teachings of the Dutch theologian Arminius. Although Arminius himself was dead by 1618, a meeting was held that year and the following year at Dordrecht in Holland. This came to be known as the Synod of Dort.

The Synod of Dort concluded the truth of five teachings of John Calvin—that came to be remembered by the acronym TULIP. This particular scheme of five teachings or "points" was not derived from John Calvin at all but formulated to refute five points in which Arminius disagreed with Calvin. The five have nevertheless come to define Calvinism for many.

1. Total Depravity (T)
   Is mankind basically good or basically depraved? Calvin wrote in the *Institutes*, "The mind of man is so completely alienated from the righteousness of God that it conceives, desires, and undertakes everything that is impious, perverse, base, impure, and flagitious. His heart is so thoroughly infected by the poison of sin that it cannot produce anything but what is corrupt; and if at any time men do anything apparently good, yet the mind always remains involved in hypocrisy and deceit, and the heart enslaved by its inward perversity."[1]

2. Unconditional Election (U)
   Did man not choose to believe and determine his own salvation? In the *Institutes* Calvin wrote, "In conformity, therefore, to the clear doctrine of Scripture, we assert that by an eternal and immutable counsel God has once for all determined both whom He would admit to salvation, and whom He would condemn to destruction. We affirm that this counsel, as far as concerns the elect, is founded on His gratuitous mercy, totally irrespective of human merit; but that to those whom He devotes to condemnation, the gate of life is closed by a just and irreprehensible, but incomprehensible, judgment."[2]

3. Limited Atonement (L)

Did not Christ make salvation available for all of mankind? Calvin wrote in the *Institutes*, "It must be noted that so long as we are apart from Christ and separated from Him, all that He has done and suffered for the salvation of the human race is useless and of no importance." This the Synod interpreted as atonement limited to believers only.[3]

4. Irresistible Grace (I)

Did man not attain salvation by exercising his free will and receiving grace? No, according to Calvin in the *Institutes*: "The Apostle teaches not only that grace to will the good is offered us if we will accept it, but that God makes and forms that will within us, which is to say no other thing than that God by His spirit trains, inclines, moderates our heart, and that He rules it as His own possession."[4]

5. Perseverance of the Saints (P)

Can the elect fall from grace and lose salvation? No, Calvin assured readers of the *Institutes* that God "not only promises to give a new heart to His elect so that they may walk according to His precepts, but that they may walk therein in fact."[5] The effect is lasting. "The Spirit of God, being consistent with Himself, nourishes and confirms in us the love of obedience that He instilled into us from the beginning."[6]

195

The Synod of Dort believed the first four of these five points were interdependent. The acceptance of one required the acceptance of all four. Serious theologians have debated these five conclusions and their foundation in Calvin's *Institutes* for hundreds of years. Those who hold to the conclusions of the Synod of Dort are called "hard-line Calvinists." Those who have modified those conclusions Norman Geisler called "Moderate Calvinists." In *Chosen But Free,* published in 1999, Geisler argued the following—based more on the Bible than the *Institutes*—for each of the five points.

1. Total depravity: Moderate Calvinists believe that unsaved people are not so depraved that they do not understand the truth of Christianity. This contrasts to the synod's conclusion that mankind's depravity renders it incapable of understanding the truth.

2. Unconditional election: Moderates believe that election is unconditional from the standpoint of God, but it requires one condition on the part of the receiver: faith. The Synod concluded election was entirely unconditional.

3. Limited atonement: Moderate Calvinists believe Christ atoned the sins of everyone, but only the believers, or the "elect," are redeemed by His sacrifice. In other words, the atonement is limited in extent for the synod, whereas the atonement is limited by result for the Moderates.

4. Irresistible grace: Moderates believe irresistible grace works on all who are willing, all who are receptive. In other words, God's grace is persuasive rather than compulsive.

5. Perseverance of the saints: Moderate Calvinists believe that saints may well die in sin, but they are not lost. In other words, once "elected" the elect, though imperfect enough to sin, cannot fall completely from grace.

These five conclusions of the Moderates presented by Geisler are much more widely accepted by "Calvinists" of the twenty-first century than those discussed above for the Synod of Dort. Followers of chiefly the Reformed and Presbyterian churches are only too aware of these controversies. Many refer to their own beliefs in terms of how many of the five points they believe. So, some call themselves "three-point Calvinists" or "four-point Calvinists" and so forth. Amazingly, according to Geisler, Calvin himself would have been a four-point Calvinist using the Synod of Dort as a basis. Geisler insisted Calvin did not believe in Limited Atonement.

It is a major irony John Calvin is usually remembered for predestination. As the German scholar Paul Wernle said, "It cannot be over-emphasized: faith in predestination is a long way from being the center of Calvinism; much rather is it the last consequence of faith in the grace of Christ in the presence of the enigmas of experience."[7] Election and predestination were not cornerstones of Calvin's *Institutes*. He considered the concepts logical outgrowths of his complete development of Christianity from the Bible.

Even the much-used TULIP construct falls far short of what Calvin wrote of Christianity. Calvin is surely the most misunderstood theologian of history. He held many of the same interpretations of the Bible as the later Augustine in the fifth century and Martin Luther in the sixteenth century. Yet critics revile John Calvin alone for the supposed unfairness of divine election and predestination. Critics even hold John Calvin responsible for Puritanism, although he wrote against asceticism. Calvin's undeserved notoriety is understandable among ignorant people and modern libertines. But his notoriety among supposedly objective scholars is stunning. On the subject of John Calvin, the historian/philosopher Will Durant ranted angrily: ". . . We shall always find it hard to love the man who darkened the human soul with the most absurd and blasphemous conception of God in all the long and honored history of nonsense."[8]

John Calvin was far more rational on the subject of predestination than secular scholars like Durant:

> *Some people urge that the subject of predestination should rarely, if ever, be mentioned and tell us to avoid any discussion of it like the plague. Although they are right in saying that such deep things should be treated with moderation, the natural mind is going to raise questions. To hold a balanced view we must turn to God's Word, where we shall find true understanding. Scripture is the Holy Spirit's school where everything we need to know is taught and where nothing is taught that is unnecessary. It would be quite wrong to keep*

*believers from the scriptural doctrine of predesti-
nation. We would deprive them of God's blessing
and scorn his Spirit. . . .[9]*

Yet to scholars obsessed by the subject, Calvin warned:

*The subject of predestination, which is difficult
enough already, is made even more puzzling and
dangerous by human curiosity. This cannot be
held back from forbidden areas, even floating up
to the clouds in a determination to discover all the
secret things of God. When we see decent men
rushing into such presumption, we must point out
how wrong it is. First, when they delve into the
question of predestination, they must remember
that they are probing the depths of divine wisdom,
and if they dash ahead too boldly, then instead of
satisfying their curiosity they will enter a maze
with no exit!. . . If we seriously consider that the
Word of the Lord is the only guide to our understanding of Him, it will prevent all presumption.
We shall realize that the moment we go beyond the
limits of Scripture, we shall be off course, in the
dark and stumbling.[10]*

"Nothing is taught that is unnecessary," John Calvin
wrote calmly of his *Institutes*. Paragraphs later—as if
anticipating future critics like Durant—he concluded, "I
shall not bother to refute some of the stupid ideas men have
raised to overthrow predestination. . . ."[11]

SUGGESTED FURTHER READING

Bainton, Roland H. *The Reformation of the Sixteenth Century.* Boston: Beacon Press, 1952.

Beza, Theodore. *The Life of John Calvin.* Sixteenth century.

Bonnet, Jules, ed. *Letters of John Calvin.* UK: Banner of Truth Trust (English translation of portions of 1855–57 French edition), 1980.

Cottret, Bernard. *Calvin: A Biography.* Grand Rapids, Michigan: Wm. B. Eerdmans, 2000.

Durant, Will. *The Reformation.* Vol. 6 of *The Story of Civilization.* New York: Simon and Schuster, Inc., 1957.

Ganoczy, Alexandre. *The Young Calvin.* Philadelphia: Westminster Press (English translation of 1966 book in German), 1987.

Geisler, Norman. *Chosen But Free.* Minneapolis: Bethany House, 1999.

Lane, Tony, and Hilary Osborne, eds. *The Institutes of Christian Religion,* Grand Rapids, Michigan: Baker Book House, 1986.

Parker, T. H. L. *Calvin: An Introduction to His Thought.* Louisville: Westminster/John Knox Press, 1995.

---. *Calvin's Doctrine of the Knowledge of God.* Grand Rapids, Michigan: Wm. B. Eerdmans, 1952.

---. *John Calvin: A Biography.* Philadelphia: Westminster Press, 1975.

Walker, Williston. *John Calvin, the organiser of reformed Protestantism, 1509–1564.* New York, London: G. P. Putnam's Sons, 1906.

Wendel, Francois. *Calvin: Origins and Development of His Religious Thought.* New York: Harper and Row, 1963.

Chapter 1

¹ T. H. L. Parker, *John Calvin: A Biography,* (Philadelphia: Westminster Press, 1975), p. 2.

Chapter 2

¹ Arthur Cushman McGiffert, *Martin Luther: The Man and His Work,* (New York: The Century Company, 1910), p. 81.
² Will Durant, *The Reformation,* vol. 6 of *The Story of Civilization* (St. Louis, 1898, and London 1910), p. 339.
³ Parker, *John Calvin: A Biography,* p. 4.
⁴ Ibid., p. 3.
⁵ Roland H. Bainton, *Here I Stand: A Life of Martin Luther,* (New York: Abingdon Press, 1950), p. 50.

Chapter 3

¹ Parker, *John Calvin: A Biography,* p. 6.
² Bernard Cottret, *Calvin: A Biography,* (Grand Rapids: Wm. B. Eerdmans Publishing Company, 2000), p. 12.
³ Ibid., p. 14.
⁴ *Encyclopaedia Britannica,* 15th ed., 2001, s.v. "Francis I."
⁵ Ibid.
⁶ Durant, *The Reformation,* p. 493, quoting L. Batiffol, *Century of the Renaissance,* 1935, p. 44.
⁷ Durant, *The Reformation,* p. 285.
⁸ Ibid., p. 284.

Chapter 4

¹ Cottret, *Calvin: A Biography,* p. 17.
² Durant, *The Reformation*, p. 509.
³ Ibid., pp. 509–10.
⁴ Ibid., p. 512.
⁵ Ibid., p. 365.
⁶ Ibid.
⁷ Preserved Smith, *The Life and Letters of Martin Luther,* (New York: Houghton Mifflin Company, 1911, 2d ed.,1914), p. 158.
⁸ Ibid., p. 159.

Chapter 5

¹ Francois Wendel, *Calvin: Origins and Development of His Religious Thought,* (New York: Harper and Row, 1963), p. 21, quoting John Calvin's *Commentary on the Psalms.*

[2] Kelly DeVries, *Joan of Arc: Military Leader,* (UK: Sutton Publishing, 1999), p. 79.

[3] Jules Bonnet, ed., *Letters of John Calvin,* (UK: Banner of Truth Trust, abbreviated English translation of 1855–57 edition in French, 1980), p. 32.

[4] Theodore Beza, *The Life of John Calvin.,* Sixteenth century.

[5] Parker, *John Calvin: A Biography,* p. 16.

[6] Wendel, *Calvin: Origins,* p. 22.

[7] Ibid., p. 20.

[8] Ibid.

[9] Parker, *John Calvin: A Biography,* p. 18.

[10] Durant, *The Reformation,* p. 497.

[10] Ibid., p. 498.

[11] Parker, *John Calvin: A Biography,* p. 20.

[12] Williston Walker, *John Calvin, the organiser of reformed Protestantism, 1509–1564,* (New York, London: G. P. Putnam's Sons, 1906), p. 21.

[13] Ibid.

Chapter 6

[1] Parker, *John Calvin: A Biography,* p. 26

[2] Wendel, *Calvin: Origins,* p. 32.

[3] Parker, *John Calvin: A Biography,* p. 163.

[4] Ibid., p. 24.

[5] Bonnet, *Letters of John Calvin,* pp. 32–33.

[6] Parker, *John Calvin: A Biography,* p. 29.

[7] Durant, *The Reformation,* p. 505.

[8] Ibid., p. 500.

Chapter 7

[1] Parker, *John Calvin: A Biography,* p. 33.

[2] Ibid., p. 163.

[3] Durant, *The Reformation,* pp. 461–62.

[4] *Encyclopaedia Britannica,* 15th ed., 2001, s.v. "Nicene Creed," and many other sources.

[5] Parker, *John Calvin: A Biography,* p. 35.

[6] Ibid., p. 36.

[7] Ibid., p. 37.

[8] Ibid., p. 38.

[9] From Luther's Catechism (public domain) and many other sources; note that Catholic version says "Holy Catholic Church."

[10] Parker, *John Calvin: A Biography,* p. 39.
[11] Ibid.
[12] Ibid.
[13] Ibid., p. 41.
[14] Ibid.

Chapter 8

[1] Parker, *John Calvin: A Biography,* p. 42.
[2] Ibid.
[3] Ibid.
[4] Ibid., p. 43.
[5] Ibid.
[6] Ibid., p. 44.
[7] Ibid., p. 46.
[8] Ibid.
[9] Ibid.
[10] Ibid., p. 47.
[11] Ibid.
[12] Ibid.
[13] Ibid., pp. 47–48.
[14] McGiffert, *Martin Luther: The Man and His Work,* p. 29.
[15] Ibid., p. 31.
[16] Parker, *John Calvin: A Biography,* p. 48.
[17] Ibid., p. 49.
[18] Wendel, *Calvin: Origins,* p. 133.
[19] Durant, *The Reformation,* p. 463.

Chapter 9

[1] Parker, *John Calvin: A Biography,* p. 53.
[2] Ibid.
[3] Ibid.
[4] Ibid.
[5] Ibid., pp. 58–59.
[6] Ibid., p. 64.

Chapter 10

[1] Parker, *John Calvin: A Biography,* p. 66.
[2] Ibid.
[3] Bonnet, *Letters of John Calvin,* p. 46 n.
[4] Ibid.
[5] Ibid., p. 50.

[6] Ibid.

[7] Parker, *John Calvin: A Biography,* p. 69.

[8] Ibid., p. 67.

[9] Ibid., p. 69.

[10] Ibid., p. 71.

[11] Norman Geisler, *Chosen But Free,* (Minneapolis: Bethany House, 1999), p. 150.

[12] Ibid., p. 151.

[13] Ibid.

[14] Ibid.

[15] Ibid., p. 164.

[16] Ibid., p. 151.

[17] Ibid., p. 165.

[18] Ibid., p. 166.

[19] Ibid., p. 167.

[20] Ibid.

[21] Ibid., pp. 167–68.

[22] Ibid., p. 170.

[23] Ibid., p. 171.

[24] Ibid., p. 162.

Chapter 11

[1] Parker, *John Calvin: A Biography,* p. 72.

[2] Ibid.

[3] Ibid., p. 73.

[4] Durant, *The Reformation,* p. 464.

[5] Ibid.

[6] Parker, *John Calvin: A Biography,* p. 73.

[7] Ibid.

[8] Durant, *The Reformation,* p. 470.

[9] Parker, *John Calvin: A Biography,* p. 71.

[10] Ibid., p. 78.

[11] Ibid.

[12] Durant, *The Reformation,* p. 471.

[13] Parker, *John Calvin: A Biography,* p. 79.

[14] Ibid., pp. 79–80.

[15] Ibid.

[16] Ibid., p. 82.

[17] Ibid., p. 85.

[18] Ibid., p. 86.

[19] Ibid.

[20] Ibid., p. 91.
[21] Ibid., p. 92.
[22] Ibid., p. 93.
[23] Ibid., p. 94.
[24] Ibid., p. 84.
[25] Ibid., p. 85.

Chapter 12

[1] Parker, *John Calvin: A Biography,* p. 88.
[2] Ibid., p. 87.
[3] Bonnet, *Letters of John Calvin,* p. 25.
[4] Parker, *John Calvin: A Biography,* p. 101.
[5] Ibid., p. 103.
[6] Ibid.
[7] Ibid., p. 104.
[8] Ibid.
[9] Bonnet, *Letters of John Calvin,* pp. 71–72.
[10] Ibid., p. 71.
[11] Ibid., pp. 73–74.
[12] Parker, *John Calvin: A Biography,* p. 108.
[13] Ibid.
[14] Durant, *The Reformation,* p. 485.
[15] Parker, *John Calvin: A Biography,* p. 100.
[16] Ibid., p. 110.
[17] Ibid., pp. 103–4.
[18] Ibid., p. 110.
[19] Bonnet, *Letters of John Calvin,* p. 105.
[20] Ibid.
[21] Ibid., p. 107.
[22] Ibid.
[23] Ibid., pp. 104–5.
[24] Ibid., p. 105.

Chapter 13

[1] Parker, *John Calvin: A Biography,* p. 130.
[2] Ibid., p. 113.
[3] Ibid.
[4] Ibid., p. 118.
[5] Ibid., p. 102.
[6] Bonnet, *Letters of John Calvin,* p. 105.

Chapter 14

  [1] Bainton, *Here I Stand: A Life of Martin Luther,* p. 50.
  [2] Bonnet, *Letters of John Calvin,* pp. 242–43.
  [3] Parker, *John Calvin: A Biography,* pp. 151–52.
  [4] Ibid., p. 155.
  [5] Ibid., p. 153.
  [6] Ibid., pp. 153–54.
  [7] Ibid., p. 155.

Chapter 15

  [1] Durant, *The Reformation,* p. 463.
  [2] Ibid., p. 464.
  [3] Wendel, *Calvin: Origins,* p. 234.
  [4] Ibid., p. 273.
  [5] Ibid., p. 245.
  [6] Ibid.
  [7] Ibid., p. 265, quoting a translation of Paul Wernle, *Der evangelische Glaube noch dem Hauptschriften der Reformatoren, V. III: Johann Calvin,* 1919, p. 403.
  [8] Durant, *The Reformation,* p. 490.
  [9] Tony Lane and Hilary Osborne, eds., *The Institutes of Christian Religion,* (Grand Rapids: Baker Book House, 1986), pp. 215–16.
  [10] Ibid., pp. 214–15.
  [11] Ibid., p. 216.